Greenwich Readers

Education & Training for Life

Language, Communication and Learning

This Reader is one of a series designed to support teachers and trainers in the post-compulsory sector of education. It will be of value to those who are working in colleges of further and higher education, sixth form colleges, adult and community education institutes, training units, and institutions of specific vocational preparation in the health service, the police service and the armed forces. The topics have been selected to represent a wide view of currently important issues and, by providing appropriate material for critical reflection on professional practice, the book will meet the needs of experienced teachers and trainers as well as those in the earlier stages of their careers.

In addition to such general use, the volume is one component of an integrated Certificate in Education/Postgraduate Certificate in Education course offered by the School of Post-Compulsory Education and Training at the University of Greenwich. Further information on this and other programmes of study and related academic services may be obtained from:

School of PCET
University of Greenwich
30 Park Row
London SE10 9LS

telephone: 020 8331 9230
fax: 020 8331 9235
e-mail: pcet@gre.ac.uk
www.gre.ac.uk

The planned range of titles in this series is as follows:

- Adult Learners, Key Skills & the Post-16 Curriculum
- Equality, Participation & Inclusive Learning
- Flexible Learning & ICT
- Language, Communication & Learning
- Perspectives on Learning
- Planning Teaching & Assessing Learning
- Professionalism, Policies & Values
- Supporting Students

Enquiries about the current availability of these publications should be addressed to the School Office at the above address.

Tony Lewis
Series Editor

Language, Communication and Learning

A Reader

Maude Gould

Published in 1999 by Greenwich University Press and prepared for publication by:

Procurement and Business Services Department
University of Greenwich
Woolwich Campus
Wellington Street
London
SE18 6PF

ISBN 1 86166 072 3

Cover designed by Pete Birkett

Text design and layout by Christine Murray

In the majority of cases the contents of the readings and extracts in this volume have been reproduced as they appear in the publications from which they have been taken.

Every effort has been made to trace all the copyright holders, but if any have inadvertently been overlooked the publishers will be pleased to make the necessary arrangements at the earliest opportunity.

University of Greenwich, a charity and a company limited by guarantee, registered in England (reg no 986729). Registered Office: 30 Park Row, Greenwich, London SE10 9LS.

Contents

Acknowledgements

Acknowledgement is made for permission to reproduce the extracts quoted:

Burton G & Dimbleby R (1995) *Between ourselves: an introduction to interpersonal communication* 2nd edn Arnold: pp101–105

Fairclough N (1989) *Language and power* Longman: pp43–49, 64–65

Hardman F & Williamson J (1998) 'The discourse of post-16 English teaching' *Educational Review*, 50 (1), pp5–14

Harkin J & Davis P (1996) 'The communication styles of teachers in post-compulsory education' *Journal of Further and Higher Education* 20 (1) Spring: pp25–34

Hayes N (1994) *Foundations of psychology: an introductory text* Routledge: pp104–112, 514–527

Hoadley-Maidment E (1994) 'Language support issues in Access courses' *Journal of Access Studies* 9 (1) Spring: pp61–62, 66–71, 74–77

Minton D (1991) *Teaching skills in further & adult education* City & Guilds and Macmillan: pp175–184, 187–195

Montgomery M (1995) *An introduction to language and society* 2nd edn Methuen: pp93–98

Powell M & Solity J (1990) *Teachers in control: cracking the code* Routledge: pp92–106

Sacks O (1989) *Seeing voices* Picador: pp37–45, 61–64, 73–75

Target F (1995) 'Cultural and linguistic factors in assessment' in P Toogood ed *Assessment issues in further education* Coombe Lodge Report 24 (10) Further Education Development Agency: pp925–937

Wallace W (1997) 'With an 'uh uh' here and a mutter there' *The Times Educational Supplement* (4202) 10.1.97 TES 2: pp4–5

The School of Post-Compulsory Education and Training

The School of PCET, as it is known, has its origin in Garnett College in London, one of three institutions set up by the Ministry of Education in the late 1940s for the initial training of technical college lecturers. After many developments and organisational changes over the past 50 years, its future within the University of Greenwich will be from a campus on the banks of the River Thames in Christopher Wren's former Royal Naval College.

The School's services and students, though, are not only locally based, but nationwide and international. PCET is a leader in distance provision for lecturers, trainers, administrators and other support staff from all sectors of post-school provision, as well as from the public services and voluntary and commercial training organisations. It has associated centres in various parts of the United Kingdom, and there are projects in China, South Africa and Russia, and leadership of research and information networks within the European Union.

We aim, in both our teaching and our research, to relate professional practice to learning theory and current policy issues. This permeates all of the School's programmes – from initial training on Cert Ed/PGCE programmes, through professional development at BA/BSc and Masters levels and the work of our Training and Development Office, to our portfolio of short courses and bespoke in-house provision. There is a thriving group of research students, and the School has been at the forefront of innovation in computer mediated communication. We provide a comprehensive service for further, higher and adult education, helping people to help others learn through life.

Ian McNay
Head of School

Maude Gould now divides her time between working in the Open Learning Centre at a further education college and running the BA/BSc Education and Training programme at the University of Greenwich. Previously, she taught for many years in a variety of institutions before becoming staff development co-ordinator at an inner London college.

Introduction

The issue of communication between teachers and their learners is addressed to some degree in most of the standard general textbooks on the education of young people at school. It is an area of study which has acquired greater significance in recent years, as teaching in all phases and sectors of education has become less formal and has thus offered fewer established pedagogical and linguistic conventions for teachers to fall back on. At the same time, the widening of participation in education and training makes demands on teachers to minimise the barriers to communication which arise from specialist language and vocabulary and from the presence in many of our schools and colleges of significant numbers of young people who do not speak English at home.

In adult and community education, interpersonal relationships have traditionally been characterised by a relaxed and informal dialogue between tutors and students. However, in other areas of vocational education and training, developments in the practice of teaching – and thus in the strategies of communication – have been stimulated by changes in the culture of our society, in particular:

- the implementation of equal opportunities policies, which have broadened access to education and training
- current initiatives to address the inclusion of people with learning difficulties and disabilities
- recent developments in the technology of communications media.

These have all had implications for the nature of teacher-learner communication and discourse, and have reinforced the view that language is not the concern only of the specialist language teacher.

The contributions to this Reader have been chosen to help in exploring the language used by teachers, by students, and by all who work within institutions of post compulsory education and training. The extracts have been arranged into four sections, corresponding to four major areas in the study of language in education: the communication and cultural experience of the student; the recognition of language varieties; the role of the teacher; and issues of teaching strategy.

The volume begins with a set of extracts which focus attention on the learner, first looking at selected theories of the place of language in the development of cognitive processes and in the expression of culture and meaning, and then considering the implications of identifying and supporting the language needs of adult learners and designing appropriate ways in which learning can be assessed.

The following section looks at the variety of languages and language modes and registers used by learners, including language which does not arise from speech.

These are related to significant aspects of individual and group experiences and to the perceptions and prejudices with which teachers have to work.

The third section presents a general analysis of the nature of language and the uses of language as part of the teacher's total repertoire of skills. Each extract is robust in its approach, stressing the responsibility of the teacher to be a precise user of language, and one who is aware of the factors that affect meaning and of those that may impede communication.

The final section contains four perspectives on communication issues in the activity of teaching. One is a report on research into the communication styles of teachers in post compulsory education; the second derives some general conclusions about classroom language from the teaching of literature; the third is an analysis of the role that language plays in the assertion of power relationships, such as those between teachers and students; the final contribution to this volume explores the important aspects of communication which are not dependent upon the use of language.

Teaching is a dynamic activity, a puzzle and a challenge; the sensitive use of language is at the core of this activity. These readings should help to illuminate individual practice and to provide opportunities for reflection on the role of language in the planning and managing of learning.

Maude Gould
May 1999

Language, Culture and Meaning

The main principle underpinning the professional activity of teaching is that the potential which people have can be turned into achievement, given appropriate instruction, guidance and support. The process is most successful when there is the least gap between a learner's current attainment and their intended goals, and where we have the smallest number of new skills or change factors to be accommodated in the learning process. The traditional transition from school VIth form to undergraduate study might be seen to be an example of this. However, current preoccupations relating to widening participation in post-school education and training to groups previously un- or under-represented, together with a commitment to providing equality of opportunities for success, present a challenge for teachers and trainers. We need to recognise that our role is not only concerned with facilitating learning in our own subject specialism or area of vocational expertise, but also in supporting and extending the study skills which our students have to acquire and use. The most important of these skills is concerned with communication and the use of language.

There is much research which explores the relationship between language, thought and the formation of concepts, and which claims to illuminate the different ways of thinking and the different sorts of cognitive processes which we observe in individuals, in cultures, and in specific socio-economic, gender and other groupings. But a number of significant questions remain to puzzle the teacher, including:

- is the way we think defined by the language that we have at our disposal?
- how far is the language that we use culturally determined?
- is proficiency in language a part of general intellectual ability?
- do we over-emphasise such proficiency in the way we assess the performance of students?
- if education is principally mediated through language, whose language should we be using?
- in what way does written language differ from spoken language?
- are there significant aspects of communication that lie outside the framework of language?

If our academic conventions about the presentation of knowledge and the validation of experience are based on a set of rules and practices which relate to the intellectual development and understanding of one group in society but are not universal, then we have a problem. How are we to make these conventions of the 'learning culture' accessible to all our students, not just those who are already familiar with them?

Theories of 'verbal deprivation' make judgements about the inability of students from some social groups to thrive in an academic setting to which – it is claimed – they bring an impoverished use of vocabulary and structure. As a result, teachers may find themselves worrying about the capacity of some of their students to be successful academically for reasons which are not to do with their innate ability or their aptitude in the subject they are studying. We have to recognise the status of the language codes and registers of different categories of student, and may need to re-think what guidance and support means, involving a redefinition of our specialism and the renegotiation of our expectations of those who teach it.

We ourselves will not necessarily have learned, or learned to analyse, the language conventions which we have been able to use in the process of acquiring our own qualifications and expertise. As with all forms of communication, performing in one's own field is very often something which has become automatic, not least in our familiarity with the specialist language of the subject. We may see our main occupation as teachers and trainers as passing on the concepts and skills of our subject specialism; but there is a language dimension to the studying of that specialism that we must not ignore if we wish our students and trainees to make the transition from potential to achievement.

1.   Language and Thinking

Nicky Hayes

The way that language interlinks with other cognitive processes has been a central focus of investigations into language for many years. The early behaviourists had argued that thinking was little more than *sub-vocal speech*: infinitesimal movements of the larynx and the throat, which had become so habitual that the person no longer noticed that they were happening. But some forms of thinking don't involve language at all: in a study on concept formation, Humphrey (1951) showed that if people were asked to identify the concept linking a series of cards which were turned over one at a time, they would generally find that they could select the right card long before they could articulate the rule that they were following. It was apparent, then, that some forms of cognitive representation could take place without language.

Bruner (1964) proposed that language is the most important system of cognitive representation that we possess. By using words as symbols to represent ideas, we find it much easier to develop classifications and general or abstract concepts. This means that we can structure our experience and understand connections between different experiences much more easily than we could with a more limited system of representation, such as that available to other animals. Bruner's emphasis on the value of language as a means of representation expresses a popular idea about the relationship between language and thinking...

Language and culture

One of the best-known theories about the relationship between language and thinking is sometimes known as the *Sapir–Whorf hypothesis*, because it was developed by the American linguist and anthropologist Edward Sapir and his pupil Benjamin Lee Whorf, and sometimes as the *linguistic relativity hypothesis*. In its strongest form it includes the idea of *linguistic determinism*. This is the idea that language determines thinking: if there is no way to represent a concept in a language, then that concept is not available for people who speak that language.

The Sapir–Whorf hypothesis was stated in its strong form by Sapir in 1947. His idea was that each individual is cognitively dependent on their language system, in the sense that the categories and distinctions which are encoded in that language will determine the kind of thinking which someone is capable of. In addition (the 'linguistic relativity' part of the theory) each language system has its own unique set of such categories and distinctions, different from other languages. According to Sapir, this meant that it would never really be possible to translate an idea perfectly from one language to another.

Cultural relativity

In 1911, Boas had shown how different languages often involve distinctions which are special to the particular language. One of his most famous examples was that of an

Eskimo language which had twenty-seven different words for snow — illustrating how the language, environment and culture of a people were interlinked. However, such examples don't necessarily show that language determines thought, since they could equally well be taken to show that the environment causes language. In practice, neither Sapir nor Whorf subscribed completely to the strong form of the linguistic relativity hypothesis. Instead they adopted a weaker form, which simply stated that language could be influential in affecting the kind of thinking which people usually engaged in.

One of several examples given by Whorf (1956) was that Hopi Indians used the same word for 'insect', 'air-pilot' and 'aeroplane'. He argued that this showed how underlying patterns of thought within that culture were different from Europeans, since European thinking couldn't perceive connections between these three different things. But this argument has been heavily criticised: for example, Greene (1975) pointed out that the same word, 'drive', is used in English to mean a number of different things: operating a motor vehicle, playing a golf stroke, a wide pathway leading to a house, an intense ambition, etc.; but that doesn't mean that speakers of English see the connection between all the different meanings. Inferring cognitive patterns from linguistic data can lead to misleading impressions.

There is, however, a certain amount of supporting evidence for the weaker form of the linguistic relativity hypothesis. Farb (1974) studied Japanese women living in San Francisco who had married American servicemen. They spoke English to their husbands and children, but Japanese with each other. When they were interviewed in both languages, it was found that the attitudes that they expressed differed markedly depending on the language which was used. For instance, when they were asked to complete the statement: 'When my wishes conflict with my family's...', in Japanese they said '...it is a time of great unhappiness', but in English they said '...I do what I want.' Farb explained this in terms of the 'language world' of cultural ideas and assumptions that was generated by using the language: the women expressed attitudes appropriate to the language world that they were inhabiting when they spoke.

...Bruner's idea of language as the vehicle for categorisation and conceptualisation also implies that people will tend to notice and remember things which are easily codable in their language. The English language, for example, has a large number of words for writing and drawing implements (such as pen, biro, pencil, etc.), with the consequence that we can make subtle distinctions in these, which someone from a non-literate culture might regard as entirely unnecessary. After all, they all make marks on pieces of paper!

However, even if a language doesn't have specialist words, languages can be adapted and developed when the need arises. The English language, for instance, has no single word for a way-of-looking-at-the-world, but it imports the German word *Weltanschauung* for this purpose. English may not have twenty-seven different words for snow, but skiers have developed several ways of describing different kinds of snow, despite the limitations of the language. Most groups with an occupational focus tend to develop specific vocabularies which allow them to refer to finer details of their occupation than might otherwise have been possible: this is the purpose of specialist 'jargon', for instance.

Another problem with the idea that language determines thought is its corollary: that everyone who speaks the language will therefore tend to think in similar ways. Within a particular language-speaking culture there are often subcultures, each of which may be very different from one another, and sometimes people belonging to these subcultures have very different ways of seeing the world despite speaking the same language.

The verbal deprivation hypothesis

The *verbal deprivation hypothesis* is a theoretical approach which also arises from the view that thinking is dependent on language; or at least, sophisticated forms of thinking like abstract reasoning and classification are. This implies that variations in language ability will produce variations in how capable language users are of thinking in sophisticated ways. The verbal deprivation hypothesis predicts that people who for one reason or another have only a limited command of language will be less capable of sophisticated reasoning than people who have an extensive command of the same language.

One of the most well-known statements of verbal deprivation hypothesis was made by Basil Bernstein, in 1973. Bernstein was a sociologist who was particularly interested in how different kinds of knowledge are distributed throughout society. In particular, he distinguished between universalistic and particularistic orders of meaning. *Universalistic meanings* in Bernstein's terms are to do with abstract, general principles: knowledge which can be looked at independently of specific contexts. *Particularistic meanings*, on the other hand, are to do with immediate, specific ideas or examples, which are often highly dependent on the context in which they happen.

Bernstein argued that it is only by being able to perceive universalistic orders of meaning – general principles – that people can recognise the basis of their own experience, and so become able to change it. If their understanding of situations is particularistic - tied to the particular context - then they are much less able to change, because it becomes much more difficult to see alternatives. If you interpret a long-term difficulty which you are having with a supervisor at work as being a set of specific reactions to specific objects or events, it is difficult to change that situation. But if you see it as a manifestation of racism, because you come from a different ethnic background, then it is possible (though not necessarily easy) to do something about it. In the first case, the particularistic understanding ties you to the specific situations and circumstances, so there is little you can do except try to avoid trouble. In the second case, the universalistic interpretation means that you can register a formal complaint or bring other social controls into the situation.

Bernstein also argued that different forms of language use, which he initially referred to as linguistic codes, and later as socio-linguistic codes, serve to direct their users towards either universalistic or particularistic forms of meaning. Bernstein defined a 'code' as a set of principles of semantic organisation. He defined two main codes, which he called elaborated and restricted codes of language. *Elaborated language codes*, he said, allowed people access to universalistic forms of meaning, while *restricted language codes* were much more context-dependent, and so only allowed for particularistic meanings. The table [below] shows the differences which Bernstein identified between the two language codes.

Bernstein argued that the class system limits access to elaborated codes, through socialisation into language use. Working-class children, he argues, tend to encounter restricted codes of language in their home and wider social context; whereas elaborated codes are the dominant form of language used in middle-class homes. Since school knowledge tends to require the explicit use of elaborated codes, middle-class children have an automatic advantage, because 'school language' is familiar to them; whereas working-class children encounter a different form of language at school than the one that they are familiar with from their home environment, and consequently begin school with a disadvantage.

Elaborated code	*Restricted code*
Verbally explicit meaning	Verbally implicit meaning
High proportion of: subordinate clauses; the pronoun 'I'; passive verbs; uncommon adverbs; conjunctions and adjectives	High proportion of: personal pronouns, especially 'you' and 'they' and tag questions asking for agreement
Independent of extra-linguistic features (e.g. non-verbal signals, shared experience)	Relies on extra-linguistic features of communication
Context-independent	Context-dependent
Readily used to handle abstract concepts	More appropriate for concrete concepts
Expresses speaker's individuality (e.g. personal values)	Stresses speaker's membership of group, with shared assumptions
Maintains social distance	Strengthens social relationships
More common among middle-class speakers	More common among working-class speakers
Used in formal settings (e.g. academic debate)	Used in informal settings (e.g. family, friends)

Elaborated and restricted language codes
(from Bernstein 1973)

Criticisms of the verbal deprivation hypothesis

Bernstein's work carried the implicit idea that working-class children were verbally deprived: that they grew up with less verbal stimulation than middle-class children, and that the verbal stimulation which they did receive was so highly context-dependent that it tied them to particularistic meanings and didn't allow for abstract thinking. This concept of verbal deprivation was sharply challenged by Labov, in 1972, who argued that it is unrealistic as a representation of how working-class children actually learn language. Many such children, Labov argued, actually grow up in an environment with a very high level of linguistic stimulation, and participate fully in an actively verbal culture from a very young age. Although the language that they hear may be a dialect rather than a standard form, their environment is often linguistically enriched, and not deprived at all.

Labov performed a series of studies in which he showed that looking beyond the superficial forms of language use paints a very different picture. The reason why researchers often failed to grasp the abilities of restricted code users, he argued, is to do with the intimidating formal settings in which language use tends to be investigated. In a classic set of studies involving black children, Labov showed how a formal test setting – whether with a black or a white experimenter – resulted in very little verbal communication from the child. But in a situation where a black experimenter chatted informally to a child called Leon, using colloquial language and sitting on the floor sharing a packet of crisps, a very different picture emerged. Leon showed himself to be highly articulate and able to develop a complex abstract argument concerning the existence of God – one which, in fact, was more conceptually sophisticated than the argument produced by a fluent elaborated code user on a similar question.

Labov argued that elaborated code use as described by Bernstein did not really have anything to do with conceptual ability, despite the superficial appearances given by the wide vocabulary and structure. Often, he argued, the use of elaborated language involved hesitations and obscurities which covered up an underlying lack of ideas. Speakers of non-standard English, on the other hand, were often very direct and conceptually inventive, saying exactly what they meant without 'dressing it up' in lots of words. Also, Labov argued that the verbal deprivation model doesn't really look at everyday speech, and the day-to-day rules of discourse and syntax. If these rules are borne in mind, and language use is investigated in reassuring, non-formal settings, speakers of non-standard English can be shown to be very competent and sophisticated in their use of language.

Labov saw the verbal deprivation hypothesis as a dangerous myth, leading to stereotyping of children according to background and race; and to denial of the validity of different kinds of language. Other researchers agreed with this idea. Cazden (1970) argued that communicative competence was more important than linguistic competence – if someone can communicate effectively with other people, then it is unimportant what code of language they use. Wells (1979) showed that much of the research in this area is very naïve, usually only looking at just one or two extreme kinds of variation which are easily measured, like social class, and completely ignoring more complex or individual factors affecting linguistic style, like the situations and context of speech.

Labov's challenge to the verbal deprivation hypothesis was based on the assumption that access to elaborated language codes was necessary for access to universalistic orders of meaning. Labov identified this as a white, middle-class assumption, containing a hidden and patronising belief that those who did not use language in a white middle-class manner were essentially less able to think – i.e. stupid. What Labov's challenge demonstrated was that it doesn't matter what form of language people speak, they are still able to think as competently as – and sometimes more clearly than – elaborated language code users.

Labov was reflecting the linguistic school of thought which argues that there is no *a priori* reason for regarding one form of language as more valid than another. While most societies have a 'standard' form of language, spoken by the powerful élites of that society, the dialects and variants of that language spoken by other groups are as valid in terms of language structures and forms as the standard version. Although speakers of the standard form regard them as 'ungrammatical', they actually have their own internally consistent, but different, grammar. One example of this is the use of 'isn't it?' in West Indian English. This serves multiple purposes, much like the French *n'est-ce pas?* or the German *nicht wahr?*, and unlike standard English, which insists on different forms of interrogative depending on the preceding content: 'didn't you?', 'haven't they?', 'wasn't she?' etc. In linguistic terms, using 'isn't it?' as a general-purpose interrogative represents a consistent and acceptable grammatical principle for West Indian English. Just because it differs from middle-class Standard English doesn't make it wrong.

But there is another side to the verbal deprivation hypothesis, which seems to have become a baby which was thrown out with the bathwater. That is the idea that the education system, the society in general, favours speakers of elaborated language codes more than those who speak restricted codes and dialects in English. While linguistically a dialect of English may be as valid as Standard English, socially a speaker of such a dialect may be stereotyped or regarded as inferior. Labov takes the uncompromising view that society should change its judgements, so as to acknowledge the validity of restricted codes, and of dialect. But Bernstein was arguing that working-class children could be empowered by encouraging them to master both forms of English – so that they could interact with the wider or dominant culture on equal terms. There seems to be room for both arguments.

References

Bernstein B (1973) 'Social class, language and socialisation' in V Lee ed (1979) *Language development* Croom Helm/Open University

Boas LF (1911) *Handbook of American Indian languages* Smithsonian Institute

Bruner JS (1964) 'The course of cognitive growth' *American Psychologist* 19: pp1–15

Cazden C (1970) 'The neglected situation in child language research and education' *Journal of Social Issues* 25: pp35–60

Farb P (1974) *Word play: what happens when people talk* Bantam

Greene J (1975) *Thinking and language* MethuenHumphrey G (1951) *Thinking: an introduction to its experimental psychology* John Wiley

Labov W (1972) 'The logic of non-standard English' in V Lee ed (1979) *Language development* Croom Helm/Open University

Sapir E (1947) *Selected writings in language, culture and personality* University of California Press

Wells G (1979) 'Variation in child language' in V Lee ed *Language development* Croom Helm/Open University

Whorf BL (1956) *Language, thought and reality* MIT Press

2. Language Support Issues in Access Courses

Elizabeth Hoadley-Maidment

Introduction

- *'We consider study skills to be the responsibility of the subject specialists – after all they know best what is needed for their subjects.'*

- *'All Access courses receive backup communications and study skills sessions together with numeracy. This is taught by our student support unit and is additional to anything that the subject tutors may decide to include.'*

- *'The college has a long tradition of providing communications skills as well as language support for our many ethnic minority students. We offer students a range of options, depending on their needs. This includes ESOL classes for bilingual students and both timetabled and drop-in workshops on communications and study skills.'*

Three colleges in different parts of the country; three different approaches to handling the general study skills and communication skills needs of students on Access courses. The development of language and communication skills has always been addressed in Access courses, at least within the context of study skills, so it is interesting to ask why we find such a variety of approaches to their teaching. How has this come about? Is it related to the subjects that students are studying, or are the approaches simply a reflection of historical development? How far does current classroom practice take into account recent developments in the underlying academic disciplines such as linguistics and educational psychology?

This article addresses the thesis that communication skills and study skills are linked by their concern with the role of language in academic study. All education is mediated through language – this is undoubtedly a truism to professional educators, but the implications are that the acquisition of concepts, including those of a scientific or technical nature, involves language skills and that communication between student and tutor and among students as a group is a key element in the learning process. Communication in this sense encompasses both the general language that underpins academic study and the specialist language of individual academic subjects.

Initial examination of the literature shows that current approaches to the language curriculum in Access courses are the result of the interaction of several factors. These include the history of access developments in the 1970s and 1980s, the institutional context of courses, and pragmatic issues arising from these such as the availability of staff, teaching materials and classroom space. It appears that integrating developments in linguistics and language-teaching methodology has often had to take second place to policy and institutional constraints. New ideas may be implemented by individual tutors but it can be difficult to incorporate these into integrated course planning. This article sets out to examine some of these issues and poses a number of questions about curriculum design and organisation. It is hoped that it will stimulate further debate in this area...

A social and cultural framework

What is the social and linguistic context of academic study in higher education? From a sociological perspective, education may be defined as a social institution with its own values, culture, sets of rules and ways of behaving. Within this very broad category, higher education and its institutions (universities and colleges) have shared features which distinguish them from other parts of the educational system including further education. It is therefore important to prepare students for the culture that they will be entering, not just for the one in which they find themselves at present.

The culture of higher education is expressed through a combination of formal and informal rules which are shared by staff and students and which must be learned by people joining the institution. The formal rules are generally explicit: they are often written down and students are inducted into them through handbooks, by staff and in events such as Freshers' Weeks. They cover a wide range of things from course structure, assessment and accreditation systems to rules for using the library and official attitudes to absence or handing in work late.

More difficult for students to acquire are the informal 'ground rules': culturally agreed ways of behaving appropriately as a student, for example, how to behave in a seminar, what is meant by 'an essay' in different subjects, when and how to approach lecturers and tutors if you are having difficulties. These are often not made explicit to new students because it is assumed that they have learnt them further down the system. Some of the ground rules relate to the general role of 'being a student', but an important sub-category deals with the way language is used in the academic community (Sheeran & Barnes, 1990).

The term 'academic discourses' is often used to describe the ways in which different disciplines use language to create specialised communities. Students are socialised into these in order to become engineers, social scientists or art historians. This is a gradual process which is built around the learning of concepts, but central to it is the use of academic tasks to both learn the concepts and provide evidence of this learning. Tasks include such things as essays, projects, practical experiments and written examinations. All of these are highly dependent on language, including not simply everyday English but special meanings that accrue to words, expressions, grammar and so on, in order to reflect the values and meanings of specific subjects or of higher education itself.

Recent research on the nature of language use in educational settings has focused on the nature of these tasks and the kinds of text that they are expected to generate. For example, essay writing is central to many subjects. The 'university essay' expects students to present evidence and weigh it up in the form of an argument.

12

Conventions exist as to how the argument should be developed and what language should be used (Hatch, 1992). In linguistic terms, the essay as academic task and the text type required (argumentation) together form an academic genre (Kress, 1989). Academic genres are closely linked to professional ones and students must learn to use their conventions. In scientific writing, for example, the passive voice has long been used, on the basis that it creates objectivity. But learning academic discourses is not simply a question of absorbing formal language patterns. Genre-based approaches have drawn attention to the fact that, in order to produce appropriate texts, students must also consider the context of their writing and in particular the audience at whom it is directed and the purpose of the communication (Swales, 1990).

We can see, therefore, that students entering higher education must have access both to the rules, values and meanings of the culture and to the language used to express these. At the broadest level, these demands should shape the Access curriculum both in relation to core skills (providing entry to the culture of higher education as a whole) and to subject options (for entry to specific disciplines). In other words, students on Access courses are being prepared for entry to, and active participation in, a culture which is completely unknown to them. How is this best done?

A sociolinguistic approach is helpful here. Sociolinguists frequently use the term 'schema' to describe the accumulated knowledge of the world, beliefs and values that individuals bring to any communicative event. Any interaction is interpreted and understood in terms of this. But where the person is entering a new culture, their schema may not be appropriate and they will need to learn new language and behaviour rapidly if they are to function as members of this new community. It would be fair to say that, no matter what their age, everyone entering higher education for the first time lacks experience of its particular culture. Higher education generally assumes that new students will be using schema based on continuous passage through the education system, culminating in A Levels. While students proceeding direct from school will have schemas that have largely been shaped by their school experience, those of adults draw on a far wider range of life experience. Of course, further acculturation occurs during the first year of undergraduate study but, if students on Access courses are not to be culturally and linguistically disadvantaged in higher education, Access and preparatory courses need to bring them to an equal, although not necessarily identical, cultural starting point to that of school leavers. Ballard (1984) has examined this process in some detail in an Australian context and concluded that all students must make one cultural transition on entry to university, but that foreign students (in this case mostly South-East Asians and Japanese) must make both this transition and a second one because of the non-Australian culture and language that determines their schema on entry.

Transferring this to the British situation, it is apparent that adult students entering higher education through the Access route will have to make a double, or in some cases treble, cultural shift. The first shift is the one that all students must make, the second results from their 'adultness', and there is a third for those students from ethnic minority backgrounds whose language and cultural background will put them in a similar position to Ballard's foreign students (although this shift is likely to vary depending on whether or not they were born and/or received their schooling in Britain).

The shift for adults is a complex one. First, adults are mature people whose ways of learning are influenced by the fact that they occupy roles in mainstream society – as workers, parents and so forth – in a way that nineteen-year-olds do not. Second, most adult students lack confidence in their ability to study at this level because they may have been away from formal education for many years and have only modest educational achievements. Third, many Access students describe themselves as working-class and feel unsure of their ability to handle language that they associate with the middle-class. Ivanic & Simpson (1990) have shown that the language used by adults entering higher education is further from the higher education norm than that of younger students. On entering higher education, therefore, the likelihood of communication breaking down between the student and the tutor is greater for mature students. Whereas nineteen-year-olds, having spent their entire lives in the student role, will simply transfer the way they behaved last year to the new situation and, if it does not work, quickly learn by trial and error, the Access graduate may trip up by using 'inappropriate' language. Lack of confidence may further compound the problem by making them reluctant to clarify any misunderstandings.

The message for the Access curriculum is, therefore, that language issues must be addressed in a way that enables students to build up their overall confidence and to value the language they already use. At the same time, students need to broaden the range of language they have available so that they move closer to the higher education norm. It is important that they do not feel they have to unlearn ways of using language that have stood them in good stead this far. One challenge, therefore, is to enable students to use appropriate language codes, i.e. the standard English of the academic world, when in the role of student, while acknowledging that their identification with other forms of language is totally legitimate elsewhere. But because they may be firmly rooted in other dialects (or use languages other than English), Access students have to learn to use the forms appropriate to academic discourse and tasks as though they are learning a new language. Any approach to study which assumes that students already have command of complex grammatical constructions, linking devices, or a wide range of vocabulary, is limited because it is starting from the assumption that since adults may discuss complex topics fluently when speaking, they can also do so in writing. This is not necessarily the case. In linguistic terms, written text differs significantly from spoken text.

For ethnic minority students, or students studying in a second or subsequent language, this issue is even more complex. These students are making several cultural shifts:

- from adult to adult student (in common with all adult students)
- into the academic discourse (in common with all students)
- from experience of how academic discourse is organised in their culture to how it operates in British culture
- from the genres and text types of their home language and culture to those of English, e.g. the concept of 'essay' varies widely in different cultures.

The majority of ethnic minority students on Access courses will have spent some time in the British education system and will probably be more familiar with English academic genres than those of their country or culture of origin. But this is not always the case. Refugees and others who arrive here with previous experience of higher education may need to pay particular attention to cultural differences in academic settings. Even among second generation students, much informal discussion may take place in their home languages following cultural styles of debate, discussion and writing that are Indian, Chinese or French rather than English.

Implications for the Access curriculum

What are the language uses, forms and skills that Access students need to acquire? The discourses of individual disciplines and the nature of undergraduate level study demand highly complex manipulation of language. If students lack the linguistic tools (i.e. aspects of formal language), they will not be able to express the ideas they are learning (or decode them). Northedge (1992) describes in detail the way in which Access courses can tackle the learning of academic discourses by using an approach that integrates conceptual (content) learning and learning the language used by the discipline. This will take the students a long way towards the equal starting point mentioned earlier.

With adult students in general there is a world of difference between having command of language forms at recognition level and being able to use them, i.e. students can often decode, or think they can, academic-type text but they cannot manipulate it. They need to recognise that having command of standard language brings power in the academic situation. They also need to recognise that because language works as an integrated whole, people will make judgements about their overall academic ability and command of the subject matter on the basis of their use of general formal language, as much as on their command of the specialist discourse and concepts. So the acquisition of specific discourses needs to be underpinned by the development of those language elements that 'glue' the discourse together. At another level, it is important that students develop both their oral and written language skills. By the end of the Access course, students need to feel confident that they are using English in a way that will be understood by higher education tutors and by other students. While Access students sometimes fear that they will be 'picked out' as having come through the Access route, from the higher education tutor's perspective it is more often the case that no allowances will be made for their different preparation route...

Organisational issues

As we have seen, current thinking in sociolinguistics and educational theory points towards pulling together the diverse threads inherent in concepts of study skills, language support and conceptual learning. It is important that subject specialists 'own' the study skills curriculum with its aim of developing appropriate skills for handling the subject discourses. It makes sense that students develop note-taking, essay-writing and discussion skills within the context of their subject learning. However, the need to develop formal language skills points to a continuing role for the language specialist: few subject tutors consider themselves language experts and although raising their awareness of language issues may enable them to support students more effectively (Frame & Hoadley-Maidment, 1988), at the Access to Higher Education level some intensive work on formal language skills should augment the integrated programme. A particular problem exists for students following modular programmes, since they may find themselves being introduced to more than one discourse simultaneously and consequently become confused. This is a common problem in education systems based on unit-credit systems (Ballard & Clanchy, 1988) and, as credit-transfer, modular programmes and distance-learning develop in this country, one that we need to be aware of. Central language referral points may serve a useful function here, not only in relation to Access provision but also within higher education institutions. The expansion in student numbers also means rethinking the balance between the language class or workshop with face-to-face tutor support and the use of self-study approaches. There is some indication that universities are beginning to address these issues.

Conclusions

Whatever combination of approaches to language support are finally used, there is a need for all the components to feed into each other and for courses to become more of a 'seamless robe' than they have often been in the past. At present, many students perceive the language and study skills components of their courses as quite separate from the rest of the course. They need to be able to see that they use language in all their learning and that developing their language skills will improve their grasp of academic subjects. It is only in this way that they will develop the confidence to undertake the additional language-based work that university lecturers expect of students, such as reading round the subject and participating in informal academic discussions with other students; in other words becoming autonomous learners. These are the value-added output measures that Access courses should be aiming for if students are not to be disadvantaged at the next stage. We need to ask ourselves if our curriculum planning still focuses on the needs of the students when they move on into higher education, and how we ensure that the negotiation of curriculum between partner institutions operates in the changed climate of the 1990s. We need to consider whether staffing, timetabling and teaching of language and study skills simply reflects the thinking that went into initial course proposals and, if so, when this was. Perhaps it is time to re-examine the approach to language work in the light of recent educational changes: modularisation, franchising and credit transfer on the one hand but, more importantly, developments in our understanding of how language operates and its role in academic learning.

References

Ballard B (1984) 'Improving student writing: an integrated approach to cultural adjustment' in R Williams & J Swales eds *Common ground: shared interests in ESP and communication skills* (ELT Documents, 117) Pergamon, in association with the British Council

Ballard B & Clanchy J (1988) 'Literacy in the university: an "anthropological" approach' in G Taylor *et al. Literacy by degrees* SRHE and Open University Press

Frame P & Hoadley-Maidment E (1988) 'Working with subject specialists in further education – two case studies' in S Nicholls & E Hoadley-Maidment *Current issues in teaching English as a second language* Edward Arnold

Hatch E (1992) *Discourse and language education* Cambridge University Press

Ivanic R & Simpson J (1990) 'Putting the people back into academic writing' in *Literacy for the twenty-first century: proceedings of conference* Oxford University Press

Kress G (1989) *Linguistic processes in sociocultural practice* 2nd edn Oxford University Press

Northedge A (1992) *Teaching access: a tutor's handbook for the modular open-learning course, 'Living in a changing society'* Provisional edition Open University

Sheeran Y & Barnes D (1990) *School writing: discovering the ground rules* Open University Press

Swales J (1990) *Genre analysis: English in academic and research settings* Cambridge University Press

3. Cultural and Linguistic Factors in Assessment

Francesca Target

Many of the efforts to ensure equality in education have concentrated on trying to ensure that access to the system is made as widely available as possible and some excellent work has been done to increase the participation of traditionally disadvantaged groups. For example, entry requirements for courses have been re-examined and diagnostic entry procedures have been refined to allow wider access by adult returners. Access courses have been extremely successful at getting mature students into HE, in particular women and black and ethnic minority students; accreditation of prior learning has been formalised and is now widely used to enable students to enter the education system at a point appropriate to their skills and experience, and numbers in further and higher education have increased overall.

What happens though to students once they have overcome the first barrier and gained entry to a course? Little research has been done in FE but a report shows continued underachievement by black fifth-formers in external examination results (Drew & Gray, 1990). This is depressing in light of the efforts that have been made to widen access to qualifications and suggests that assessment is the key equal opportunities issue here. There are potential barriers for students at each stage of their journey through the education system, but it seems particularly fruitful to look at what happens to students once they manage to overcome the first assessment hurdle and join a programme of study. Much assessment in FE is in the form of teacher-designed tasks, projects and assignments so it is worth looking at these more closely to see if these are inadvertently presenting barriers to students. It is a particularly good time for teachers to examine assessment issues as we are currently having to rethink many of the traditional approaches in the light of the increasing emphasis on competence-based forms of accreditation, which were intended to widen opportunities for students to gain qualifications by removing 'unnecessary barriers which restrict access and progression', increasing flexibility by introducing a variety of routes to accreditation and trying to ensure access to fair and reliable assessment, free from 'overt or covert discriminatory practices' (NCVQ, 1991).

It is important to look carefully at how students are assessed in terms of the different tools which are used and to consider whether all students have equal access to the assessment tasks with which they are presented. It is also important to look at the cultural assumptions implicit in the various forms of assessment used and to question whether these may present barriers to some students. The language in which the assessments themselves are presented is also a crucial factor, as research in schools has established that the language and format of tasks can cause problems for all students and that 'This is not a problem which is restricted to low achievers, but that it can cause difficulties across the range of attainment' (Mobley, 1987). If this is true for students up to 16, it is likely that it is also true for – students over 16 in FE; in other words, linguistic factors in assessment have implications for all students so it is important to examine these in detail and to find ways in which problems can be minimised to prevent students being unintentionally disadvantaged.

The focus of this chapter, therefore, is to look in more detail at teacher-designed, on-programme assessment, for example, assignments used on BTEC and GNVQ courses, to see whether there are potential barriers for students raised by either cultural or linguistic factors and to suggest ways in which they can be avoided.

Cultural factors in assessment

Issues of culture implicit in assessment are difficult to address and it would be both foolish and naive to suggest that there could or should be such a thing as 'culture-free' assessment. By definition, everyone, teacher and student alike, is a product of their own culture and can no more remove themselves from it than they can remove themselves from the atmosphere that they breathe. This is not a problem when teachers and students come from the same cultural background and have shared assumptions about what is important and valuable in terms of skills and knowledge and the best ways to learn these. Potential problems can arise, however, when the cultural background is not shared and when one group has power over another and can impose its own set of unshared norms. This can be the case when teachers and students come from different cultural backgrounds – whether this is another class background or whether they come from different ethnic groups. Teachers, whether we like it or not and however approachable and friendly we may be, are in a more powerful position than our students as we control both access to assessment and the process itself. In other words, teachers control not only who can actually enter the system and be assessed, but what is assessed and how it is assessed. If we are not sensitive to the possibility of different assumptions, then there is potential for unfairness in both the process and outcomes of assessment. Cultural assumptions about the what and how of assessment need to be 'unpacked' and made explicit to avoid misunderstandings and to minimise possible disadvantage for groups or individuals who do not know or share the teachers' norms.

Focus of assessment

Possible issues of culture can arise at a number of levels. First there is the question of what a particular culture selects as worth assessing and whether it is knowledge or process skills or a mixture of the two. Traditional academic assessment has usually been knowledge-based and students familiar with this emphasis may be genuinely puzzled by assessment of process skills and find it difficult to understand what is being measured. For example, a black student quoted in an FEU report (unpublished) described the problem-solving aspect of assignments as, 'the English way of learning'. The student had recognised a cultural difference both in what was being assessed and the methods used, which is the first step towards gaining full access to an unfamiliar system.

The relationship between the assessment of knowledge and the assessment of process skills has been one of the issues raised during the controversy over GNVQ grading criteria, as both students and teachers had difficulty in establishing the place of underpinning knowledge within a system which graded students' work on their ability to plan, gather and handle information and to evaluate what they had done, but gave no obvious place to knowledge. In response to criticisms from a variety of quarters, the revised grading criteria now include an assessment of what the student actually knows as well as the processes that s/he engages in during the course of an assignment or project. The new fourth theme added to the grading criteria includes an assessment of 'a student's ability to synthesise knowledge, skills and understanding' (NCVQ, 1994), and has been welcomed as a recognition of the value still placed upon knowledge.

Method of assessment

Second, the method of assessment may cause problems for students. Many courses, BTEC Diplomas and GNVQs for example, both teach and assess using assignments which often focus on process skills, which could cause problems for students more used to traditional exams which value and assess knowledge. If the student (or her/his parents) is not only used to but values knowledge-based assessment in the form of exams, then s/he is unlikely to reach her/his full potential if s/he is assessed by methods which are not only unfamiliar but neither valued nor understood.

To perform well in an assessment, students need to know exactly what is expected of them, which may cause problems if assumptions about what is being looked for are not shared. For example, some systems reward the student's ability to present differently knowledge which the teacher has passed on, whereas assignment-based assessment values and rewards the student's ability to work independently. Students are expected to think and find things out for themselves, to be able to work on their own or collaboratively in groups, to plan their work and to make these plans explicit. Students may not realise this or may come from educational backgrounds which do not value these skills and abilities and, if they do not share beliefs about the value of the assessment tools being used, they have not got full access to the assessment process and are unlikely to perform well in assignments.

Context of assessment

At a more obvious level, students may have difficulty if the context in which the assessment is set is unfamiliar to them. Teacher-designed assignments, which are commonly used both to facilitate learning and for assessment purposes, often involve a series of tasks which students are asked to perform within a given context with which it is assumed they are familiar. The attempt to place tasks in a meaningful context is based upon the fact that students learn more effectively if they are able to link new and familiar knowledge and to use what they already know to help them assimilate what they do not. If the teacher-chosen context is familiar to students, then it does indeed facilitate effective learning. If the chosen context is culturally unfamiliar to some students however, then they do not have equal access to the assessment and their chances of performing well are reduced. For example, a BTEC assignment for business administration set the following context: 'You have been asked to organise a campaign to promote healthy living in your college.' On the surface this seems not to be problematic, but it assumes a shared assumption about what a healthy lifestyle involves. Students from different cultural backgrounds may not share the affluent western assumption that this involves regular exercise, cutting down on fats and consuming only moderate amounts of alcohol. For some recent arrivals to this country, or for those on very low incomes, a healthy lifestyle might involve making sure that you get enough to eat in the first place. Similarly, people coming from a professional background in which a sedentary desk job is the norm will associate exercise with leisure activities, but people with hard manual jobs may associate leisure with rest, and their health concerns may relate more to avoiding injuries or illnesses common to their occupation.

If students attempting the assignment do not share assumptions about what constitutes the key elements of a healthy lifestyle, then their access to this assignment is not the same and this may well be reflected in their different approach to it. If the teacher shares the cultural assumptions of only some of the students then this too is likely to be reflected in the marking of the work and the grades that the students get. City & Guilds (1988) suggests to its assessors that 'reference to a diversity of cultural experience is preferable to a focus upon English traditions as the acceptable modes of behaviour', and this may well be one way of making sure that particular groups of students are not consistently disadvantaged by the choice of unfamiliar contexts for assignments.

We need to be open about what is valued, taught and assessed and to avoid presenting students with unfamiliar contexts when they are being assessed. It is an important part of the teaching and learning process, of course, to familiarise students with new and different contexts and to constantly broaden and extend what they know, but this can be done as part of the learning rather than the assessment process. As teachers, it is important that we question our own assumptions, share our perceptions of the teaching and learning process with our students and are explicit about what is required and the values behind our choices.

Structure of assessment

The organisation of such scenario-based assignments can also cause problems for students. The convention is that tasks are usually done in the sequence in which they are set and each is dependent on the completion of the previous one which builds upon it. For example, a GNVQ assignment included the following tasks:

Task 1: To produce a written account of a range of research methods (observation, interview, questionnaire) detailing their advantages and disadvantages. Reference to at least one piece of existing research should be made for each method.

Task 2: Students should look in depth at the method they intend to use in Task 3 and consider carefully the suitability of the method for the topic area and the subjects. This should be presented in written form under the heading 'rationale'.

Task 3: To construct a structured questionnaire or structured interview on a topic related to a health and social care context. The research tool should contain no more than 10 questions.

On the surface, Task 3 appears the simplest and most straightforward as it does not involve reading or research and merely asks the student to produce no more than 10 questions on a topic of their choice; but it would be a mistake for the student to take what appears the easy option without having done the previous two tasks which the teacher clearly intends to impact upon it.

This intention is clear to other teachers or students familiar with this approach to an assignment, but it can be a barrier for students used to a traditional exam-based approach in which tasks can be attempted in any order, as they will have been taught to attempt their 'good' questions first. If they approach a scenario-based assignment in this way and do not use one task to build upon the other then they are highly unlikely to do well and the teacher will probably be baffled as to why the student did not attempt the tasks in the 'right' and obvious order.

As teachers and educators, we need to be aware of our own cultural assumptions about the knowledge and skills which are regarded as valuable and worth learning and passing on and, moreover, what are the ways in which these things are best learned. We also need to be aware that our assumptions about these things may be very different from our students' and we need, therefore, to share these assumptions by making them explicit. We often do this when a 'new' method of assessment is introduced; for example, most GNVQ programmes build in an induction period which provides students with the opportunity to experience unfamiliar assessment methods and to understand the rationale behind these. It is useful for students, however, if the rationale for all assessment is explained and discussed so that there is a shared understanding of what is being assessed, why and how.

Factors of language

The language used to assess is crucial as, instead of giving students access to the assessment process as intended, it can be a barrier to it for *all* students. Language is used to communicate, but it can be a potential barrier for students and the language of assessment may disadvantage both bilingual students and less able students with a limited vocabulary, as well as presenting a barrier to a higher grade for other students. The potential for miscommunication is enormous so, as teachers and assessors, we must be very clear about the language demands of any assessment tasks that we give our students: what they are expected to be able to read and understand and what they are expected to produce either orally or in writing.

The wording of instructions within an assignment is particularly problematic for students. If they are not clear about what they are expected to produce, then they do not have full access to the assessment tasks and cannot demonstrate their full potential. It is important, therefore, to look closely at areas of possible difficulty and identify some common language uses that can cause problems for students.

Formal academic language

Depending which subject is being studied and at what level, it may well be that students not only have to understand but also be able to use the formal, academic register as part of learning about their subject. If this is the case, then it needs to be explicitly taught as part of that subject as it cannot be assumed that students will necessarily already be fluent in this kind of language at the beginning of a programme of study. Students may be able to perform an assessment task competently, but will not be able to do so if they do not have access to it because they do not fully understand the language in which the task is expressed.

Assessment-specific terminology

There are conventions of the language of assessment which, as successful products of the education system, teachers have unconsciously absorbed and tend to use when writing assessments. When specifying the assessment task, we tend to use words like consider, evaluate, present, outline. Each of these instruction words implies to educated adults a particular way of presenting work in written form but, unless these conventions have been explicitly taught, many of our students may be placed at a disadvantage. Our students may well be able to perform the assessment task if they understood exactly what was expected. For example, 'Make a list of at least three points for and against,' rather than, 'Summarise the factors for and against,' or 'Present your findings in the form of a chart,' rather than, 'Present your findings appropriately'.

It is vital that we are clear about what we are assessing and that we explain this to our students. If we want our students to find out particular pieces of information, then we can assess their ability to do this by asking them to list what they have found or to complete a table filling in the appropriate gaps. It is only if we are assessing their ability to decide on the best way to present certain sorts of information that we should not specify how to present it. This is not 'helping' students in any unfair way, it is merely being clear about what we want to assess and explaining this as simply as possible to our students without relying on assumptions, conventions and understandings that may not be shared by all.

For example, instructions in a GNVQ assignment told students that 'The research tool should be piloted on a small number of appropriate subjects'. This probably meant 'Try out the questionnaire you have designed with approximately 10 suitable people'. Students may well be able to design and use a simple questionnaire, but will not have the opportunity to demonstrate this competently if they do not understand the task because they do not understand the use of non-technical words that have been used in a specialist sense. For example, in the context of this assignment, the words 'tool' and 'piloted' could cause difficulties as they 'carry a specific meaning within one subject and a different meaning in another subject or in everyday life' (Mobley, 1987). It is clear how this could cause difficulties for second-language learners, but the use of this kind of language in assessment tasks also 'discriminates against those students with poor general knowledge and/or a home environment which does not expose them to the networks of knowledge which underpin the various meanings' (Mobley, 1987). In the context of their assignment, the research tool is the questionnaire they have been asked to design and to pilot something means to try it out rather than to fly it, although this might not be instantly obvious to all students.

The introduction of competence-based forms of accreditation has brought with it a whole new set of assessment terminology like performance indicators, evidence indicators and range. Of course, this is new for teachers as well as students and it will take time to be able to use these terms meaningfully, but access to the assessment process means students have got to understand what is being assessed as well as how it is being assessed. Teachers tend to incorporate large chunks of undigested 'NVQ and GNVQ-speak' into the rubric of assessments, which can add to the problems as 'this style is far removed from the natural vocabulary and syntax of the spoken word [and] places many candidates at a disadvantage' (Mobley, 1987).

Complex sentences

Another difficulty with formal, academic language is that it uses long, complex sentences with multiple clauses which are particularly problematic if used to give students instructions about what to do in an assignment. For example, a GNVQ Advanced assignment included the following instructions: 'After reading the article, which was published by the local health authority, decide which one or two of the five recommendations for a change in diet your team wishes to research in greater detail in preparation for a publicity campaign.' This set of instructions is potentially problematic for all but the most sophisticated reader as it embeds four separate tasks within one very long sentence and it is highly likely that one or two of these may be 'missed' because the student has not registered them rather than because s/he is unable to complete them. The instructions would be much more accessible to all students if they were presented in the form of a list of tasks to be completed. For example:

- Read the article about diet.
- Make a list of the five recommended changes in diet.
- Choose two of the recommendations and research them in greater detail, using at least three sources.
- Prepare a publicity campaign to promote the two recommendations you have chosen.

Not surprisingly, long sentences are more difficult to understand than short ones, which is why sentence length is one of the factors used in measures of readability. The potential difficulty for students is compounded when complex sentences with multiple clauses are used to give instructions in an assignment as, obviously, they cannot get maximum marks or grades if only some of the tasks have been completed. The student may well be able to perform the tasks if they are clearly listed, but may not have access to them all if what is being assessed is the ability to read and understand complex text.

As previously mentioned, the language of competence-based accreditation is difficult and many teachers have complained about the extremely dense way in which performance criteria and evidence indicators are expressed. The following from the Advanced level GNVQ in Health and Social Care is typical: 'A project which evaluates a life event which threatens identity in relation to one client group (children, adolescents, adults or elders). The project should explain the role of economic and social factors in assisting individuals to cope with life event threats. Potential coping processes and methods of protecting and/or supporting individuals should be explained.' This is difficult to understand because it includes a lot of multi-syllable words, the sentences are long and complex, the passive voice is used and there is a density of subject-specific terms. The students will have to sort the information into manageable 'chunks', reorder and internalise it before they can begin to plan the project they have been asked to carry out.

It is also possible that students can miss an important instruction if it appears at the end of a long sentence, even if it is directly expressed. For example, task 1 of a BTEC Engineering assignment was: 'From your own experience, and using any advice you can get from any source – shops, magazines, catalogues, or anywhere else where information is available – draw up a list of the tools the apprentice might need.' There is a direct instruction in the last part of the sentence, but students may fail to notice it because there is so much information to take in before they get to it. The task would be more immediately accessible to the students if it came first: 'Draw up a list of tools you think an apprentice needs. Use magazines and catalogues as well as your own experience to help you.' In other words, instructions are more accessible to the students if they are placed before rather than after any supporting information or advice needed to complete the task.

If the language in which the task is presented is more complex than that needed to carry out the task itself, it is the students' ability to handle complex language that is being assessed rather than their ability to carry out the task which is nominally the focus of the assessment. It may be, of course, that the teacher does indeed wish to assess the students' linguistic abilities and this is a perfectly reasonable wish on certain courses, but the problem can arise when the teacher wishes to assess something else but does not do so because the language used in the wording of the assessment task presents barriers for students and prevents them having full access to the task itself.

Indirect instructions

A feature of formal academic English is its use of the passive voice, for example, 'It is thought that ...' rather than 'I think ...' and 'It has been shown ...' instead of 'I have shown ...'. Instructions are often given in the same form, but this can cause problems for students as they are more difficult to understand if they are indirectly expressed. For example, in the assignment quoted the instruction 'Reference to at least one piece of existing research should be made for each method' is more difficult to understand because it is expressed in the passive. It would be easier for students to pick it out as an instruction if it were written using an active verb: 'Refer to at least one piece of existing research for each method'.

Similarly, the following instructions from a BTEC assignment may not be perceived as such by all students, as they are indirectly expressed. 'When presenting both the oral and the written report, students should consider a range of visual forms of presentation including summary charts, tables, flow diagrams, photographic records, etc. In the written report these should be supported by leaflets, résumés, appendices and bibliographies.' The task would be more easily accessible to the students if they were addressed directly: 'You should present some of your information in visual form in both your oral and written report, e.g. charts, photographic records, etc'. This is another example where the language in which the task is presented is more difficult than the language needed to perform the task and what is being assessed is the student's ability to understand formal academic English rather than their ability to present an oral and written report and support this.

Informal language

Many teachers are sensitive to these problems, of course, and some excellent guidelines (Mobley, 1987 and BATD/NATE, 1989) have been produced to help those involved in the writing of examination questions. It is to avoid the problems for students which can be caused by complex, formal, academic language that teachers often use rather 'chatty', informal language when writing their own assignments. Unfortunately, this kind of language can also be problematic. For example, a GNVQ assignment told students, 'You may like to include an introduction'. What the teacher meant, of course, was 'You should include an introduction and will get a better grade if you do,' but s/he had worded it as a suggestion to make the assignment less formal and more user-friendly. The danger is that the instruction is taken literally as a suggestion and, therefore, an introduction is regarded as an optional extra. Similarly, in a BTEC assignment, students were told that 'a sketch could be useful here', and the teacher was disappointed that students did not include one when, as far as s/he was concerned, they had been told to do so. Of course, some students had taken the words literally and taken as a suggestion what was intended as an instruction expressed in informal, friendly terms.

In the same way, another BTEC Science assignment told students to 'think about the factors which affect heat loss in mammals'. Almost certainly, the teacher actually required the student not only to think about the factors but to make a list of them, but did not explicitly say so, which meant that some students did not submit any work for that part of the assignment and their grades suffered accordingly. This is a potential problem for bilingual students, who may take the instruction literally and think about the problem but not present their thoughts in written form for the assessor, but it can also cause difficulties for some native-speakers too.

Instructions worded as suggestions are a feature of middle-class speech and are readily understood by speakers with shared backgrounds. When teachers do not share the same background, however, instructions like, 'Think about the differences ...' and 'You may like to consider the costs of ...' may be taken literally as suggestions and both teachers and students may be baffled and irritated by the failure of communication. Students may feel they have completed the whole assignment and see it as unfair of the teacher to expect something extra that they were not told about, while teachers feel annoyed that students have not followed their instructions when they have made it clear what is required and, moreover, have done so in a friendly, straightforward way.

Conclusions and recommendations

As teachers and educators, we want all our students to have access to assessment, which means we need to be sensitive to the issues of culture and language discussed above. The potential for misunderstanding is enormous, even when there is a genuine wish to communicate clearly and assess fairly, so it is important to be as open and explicit as possible about what is being assessed and what exactly students need to do to demonstrate competence in a subject. This involves checking our assumptions with students and colleagues rather than assuming they are necessarily shared and it means monitoring the language we use to try to avoid introducing potential barriers for students.

If it is appropriate to assess our students' ability to handle complex language then we may do so, but when we wish to assess other skills or knowledge then we should try to ensure that the language we use does not hinder rather than help our students understand the assessment task. When designing our own assignments we can check that the context of any assignment scenario is familiar to all students and that instructions are as clear and unambiguous as possible so that what is being assessed is the students' ability to perform the task rather than their ability to comprehend it. This means avoiding the use of subject-specific vocabulary if it has not already been taught and it means being explicit about how work should be presented. 'Think about the problems ...' probably means, 'Make a list of the problems' and it is fairer to our students to make this clear. The more clearly the teacher expresses what is required of the student, the more the student has access to the assessment tasks. As teachers, we want all our students to have equal access to the education system and one way we can try to achieve this is to remove the barriers which we inadvertently present to students in the assessments we devise ourselves.

References

British Association of Teachers of the Deaf and National Association for Tertiary Education for the Deaf (1989) *Language of examinations* BATD/NATED

City & Guilds of London Institute (1988) *Guidance for the avoidance of bias* CGLI

Drew D & Gray J (1990) 'The fifth-year examination achievements of black young people in England and Wales' *Educational Research* 32(2): pp107–17 NFER-Nelson

Further Education Unit (undated) *Cultural and linguistic factors in GNVQ assessment: project report* RP814 [unpublished] FEU

Mobley M (1987) 'Making ourselves clearer: readability in the GCSE' *Working Paper 5* Secondary Examinations Council

National Council for Vocational Qualifications (1991) *NVQ notes: access and equal opportunities* NCVQ

National Council for Vocational Qualifications (1994) *GNVQ revised grading criteria* NCVQ [Three separate booklets – one for each level: foundation, intermediate and advanced.]

Varieties in Language Use

We have noted the close interactive relationship that exists between culture and language. Our society is multi-cultural in the widest sense, being an aggregation of groups which are classified by race, region, class, gender, occupation, age and so on. One significant way in which the distinctions between us are demonstrated is through the language that we use. Dialects, regional accents, slang, jargon, technical vocabulary – these are some of the most obvious manifestations of the differences. Our language helps to define our sense of identity and affirms group membership. The problem is to maintain diversity while not allowing it to erect barriers between us.

Women and men, for instance, have different vocabularies and speech patterns – usually to the disadvantage of women, which gives a particular resonance to our use of the phrase 'mother tongue'. In educational no less than other contexts communication activities can be alien to women participants. Given that teachers are often women and over half the students in our colleges are female, it may be difficult to accept that so much of the verbal and non-verbal communication is competitive, hierarchical, threatening and often demeaning to women. Although most teachers no longer make the mistake of assuming that people are all male, and are careful not to use 'he' as a universal pronoun, more sensitivity than that may be required to ensure that women and girls feel included and empowered. And this applies as much to the staff of our education and training institutions as it does to the students and trainees.

At its most extreme, language is used not simply to express 'difference from' and 'solidarity with', but also 'hostility towards'. This type of social dialect might then be described as an 'anti language'. Students, by and large, have many cultural differences from their teachers: they are usually younger, often from another social class, and sometimes from a different ethnic group. There are several dimensions along which they may feel separated, if not alienated, and they may develop with their friends a language deliberately designed to exclude others. Many adult groups, of course, do exactly the same.

This reminds teachers that they are part of a social and political structure, the effects of which cannot be ignored. Teachers should not assume that learners will trust them and share with them the values of fluency and articulacy in speech. Our 'speech community' may have little in common with theirs. Basil Bernstein, as we have seen, explained the effects of such differences in terms of what he called 'verbal deprivation'. Others have considered how far it is possible for the mind to mature at all without the benefit of language.

In the case of children born deaf it would appear that though they may not acquire speech, it is crucial for their intellectual, emotional and social growth that an appropriate variety of language be developed. In most cases this will be sign language (e.g. BSL - British Sign Language), and through this language – as with any other language – concepts and abstract thought can develop and be expressed.

4.   Language, Subculture and Gender

Graeme Burton & Richard Dimbleby

In this section we want to draw attention to ways in which language defines the diversity of subcultures, gives them meaning, incorporates and endorses their values. It is, of course, true that many aspects of subcultures contribute to this sense of distinctiveness – for example dress codes, oral traditions and visual communication. But we are not trying to make a complete case study of a culture. Rather, we are trying to make the point that culture is in one sense a product of communication, or is realised through communication. *The meaning of a culture to itself and to other cultures lies in what it says and how it says it.*

Subcultures are all around us and part of us. Just as the notion of a mass audience for the media seems to dissolve the more exactly one tries to define it, so also the notion of a British (or any other) culture tends to dissolve on examination. There are many subcultures when one considers class, region, occupation, ethnicity, youth, leisure activities, and the groups such as Hell's Angels – so many that it is as if one has to define national culture as the sum of these varied parts.

Language used by subcultures helps define their sense of identity for themselves and to others. Language used about them also defines how they are understood by the society of which they are a part. This language use by them is often about creating distinctiveness and very possibly difference from society at large. Sometimes the intention is even to deal in conflict, because conflict involving threat from without causes the group or subculture to focus protectively on its identity, its values and its survival.

In any case, identity can in cultural terms be split when for example one is speaking Punjabi at home and English at work.

In terms of distinctiveness, the language of youth cultures, for example, may involve being privy to a secondary code that refers to clothing and music through words which are not understood by the culture in general. Words even become recycled, such as the present fashion for 'fab' as a term of approval. It appeared in the Sixties, became passé in the Seventies, and is now temporarily acceptable again, with its associations of kitsch and nostalgia. Youth cultures are also marked by paralinguistic features which in Britain are notable for the adoption of the London accent (even by speakers of RP), for slurred delivery with hesitation, for appended phrases such as 'y'know' and 'sort of'.

In fact in this case the identity is mixed up with class and with a notion that borrowing certain restricted code features associates one with working class values, with something 'genuine'.

Subculture and values

Language used by and about subcultures also says things, directly or indirectly, about the values they hold and the values that others attach to them. We have just indicated that certain speech features may themselves be associated with values by referring to other factors such as class. Young Afro-Caribbeans in London have been re-using Creole forms to create a patois which serves the function of both giving them a distinct identity and enhancing their own sense of self-worth and value. And of course what they talk about is what they value. It is worth noting that what they are resisting is not only a dominant white culture in a general sense – and what is seen as a threatening police force in particular – but also previous generations of West Indian immigrants, many of whom had sought to shed their patois in order to integrate. There is a whole set of oppositions set up on the issues of age, race, authority, all of which are implicit in language. This is true in terms of language used both by subcultures and about subcultures. In this case it is worth looking at the comments we make elsewhere about discourse in the section on gender and language.

Language and gender – females

In the first place it should be said that *there are clear differences in the use of verbal and non-verbal language by men and women.* These differences not only identify the gender of the speaker, but they also say things about the nature of the interaction, the nature of the situation, and the way that each of the genders tries to deal with interactions.

The significance of these differences tends to be interpreted according to the values of the interpreter. Borisoff & Merrill (1991) say baldly that 'Numerous studies have established women's superior abilities both as decoders and encoders of verbal messages when compared with men'. Whereas Spender (1981) takes a more implicitly critical stance when she says that 'language has been made by men and used for their own purposes'.

One may also distinguish between language used by women and language used about women. Both kinds of use identify gender differences and say things about the status of women, the social behaviour of women and the conduct of relationships between the sexes.

We are, of course, talking generally about Western cultures here. But it should also be realised that other cultures may show other kinds of difference in communication, in relation to gender. Some of these differences are extreme. For example, the speech of Carib women or of Siberian females is considerably different to that of the males in many respects. There are plenty of examples of words (like some social practices) being taboo to women in other cultures.

Acquisition of gender definitions

In the first place, if a 'special language' is acquired and used by women in particular, then it must come from somewhere. The same is true of language used about women.

This language is a substantial part of the acquisition of gender definitions – what it means to be female, how one should regard females.

Females will learn to use certain kinds of talk and will learn to accept being talked to in certain ways because of their upbringing. We are talking about socialisation, about address by significant others at home and at school, about peer group talk not least in the context of games, about models of talk represented in various media. For example, there are female characteristics of hesitancy in speech and deferral to males in conversation (not universal, but frequent). Children will see these communicative behaviours represented in movies and in television drama, and so will tend to internalise and 'naturalise' this behaviour as being acceptable and normal.

Language used about women, even by women, is often demeaning and belittling. More will be said about this in the section on discourse. But, for example, it is noticeable that diminutive forms of women's names are more common for women than for men and are more commonly used even when they are older. When women are emotionally distressed it is common to hear words such as 'hysterical' or 'emotional'. These words are used to imply that they are 'not coping' or are 'out of control'. Although there is a separate issue of how emotion is expressed differently according to gender, the same kind of behaviour in men is described as anguish or outrage.

Interpersonal behaviour, language and gender

When one looks at how women use language there is evidence of *differences in non-verbal behaviour.* Females are touched more than men, they smile more and they use more eye contact. Indeed such differences are expected of them. For women the communication of gentleness, warmth, tact is seen positively. Women show more listening cues because they do more listening than men. It has also been suggested that listening is seen as a lower status, passive activity in a male-dominated world. This would tend to reinforce such behaviour. Women do of course have the difference of higher voices, but in fact some of the perceived difference is because they use a greater range of pitch than men. Females perceive, respond to and give off cues about feelings more than men. This is the more likely because this behaviour response is socially endorsed as being OK for females. In relation to talk it is more likely that women will use more of these cues because they talk more about feelings than men. Conversely, men have been found to talk about actions, and of course their related non-verbal behaviour (NVB) matches this.

This idea of a necessary connection between the two channels of communication fits in with similar points about the connections between role, relationships, perception and communication. In other words *roles create expectations about speech, which are gender specific.* Equally it can be said that gender patterns of speech represent gender roles. We make assumptions about how we expect mothers to talk, and how they talk defines them as mothers. Women are often better perceivers than men because they are better listeners: the fact that they use listening cues also elicits the information which helps them perceive others accurately. It is a kind of chicken and egg argument. The same logic applies to the fact that women disclose rather more than men (and disclosure helps improve relationships). Hargie *et al.* (1994) refer to this as well as to the work of Hill & Stull (1987) which identifies *four variables which affect disclosure by gender*. These are situational factors, strength of gender role identity, gender role attitudes, cultural gender role norms. For instance, in Western business circles there is a male-oriented view that control of emotion and of disclosure is desirable. Women who want to 'succeed' in business have to modify their usual gender role behaviour.

Generally, it has been found that men and women talk about different topics. Men tend to talk about work and sports activities. They are competitive. But women talk about family and friends and health matters. Also there is more than gender bias in the content of communication. The way women talk is also different. For example, their speech is usually more fluent and more accurate than that of males. Indeed they talk in more complex speech structure from an earlier age than do males. Argyle (1992) refers to research which identifies female characteristics such as hesitations, hedges (sort of), tags (didn't I?), and the greater use of 'doubt' words such as 'may' or 'might'. In mixed sex conversations men dominate in various ways (loudness and interruption), but also because women are in one sense more socially adroit at maintaining conversations and showing listening cues. They may, in effect, actually encourage men to talk more than they do... In terms of gender one can identify the fact that men are more verbally aggressive than women. It has also been found that people are more assertive towards those of the same gender. Other differences are numerous and subtle, and perhaps culturally defined. For example, it is less acceptable for women to use swear words than for men, though things have changed a great deal in the last generation. Women tend to use more words to amplify descriptions of experiences, not least again in respect of feelings they have had.

Female gender and discourse

A discourse may be described as a selective use of language which produces particular meanings about the subject of that discourse. These meanings may usually be described as value judgements about that subject, whether it be children, news or in this case, women. Discourses are also part of our ideology. They contribute to the total view of the world and of power relationships which are major aspects of ideology. The notion of language can apply to pictures as much as to words. But given the framework of this [book] we are concentrating on words about women and the discourse that they help create.

Miller & Swift (1979) refer to *the naming of women* as a way of implicitly demeaning them. That is to say, women are often addressed by their first names, where men are not. Women lose their names (and identity?) when they marry. Many female names are derived from male ones, but rarely has it happened the other way round. They and other writers refer to words which describe the quality of gender and draw attention to the selective nature of these words. They cite a dictionary definition which includes 'gentleness, affection and domesticity ... fickleness, superficiality and folly'. You may judge for yourself what such words say to people about the meaning of being female. In fact one can easily collect sets of words about women under headings such as appearance, occupation, sexuality, insults, and you can see that these words are largely specific to women as opposed to men. They often have *negative connotations*, or suggest some kind of limitation to female ability or potential or character. And so often such words define women in relation to men or as opposed to men. Women are 'attractive' – to men of course. And the words that are gender specific not only are used rarely about men, they may even be insults when applied to men – males don't like to be called 'pretty'.

Ironically in the light of what we have already said, part of the discourse is words about women which suggest they talk too much. Spender (1981) lists '*chatter, natter, prattle, nag, bitch, whine ... gossip*'. This language criticises and denies women talking, it devalues it. Such value-laden meanings of the discourse about femaleness extend into many areas of language use. For example, a women who is sexually charged and active may well be called a nymphomaniac. The word is not a compliment. There is no such equivalent for men, and anyway it is OK for men to be sexually active. One might even argue that simply the great number of terms identifying female clothing has a significance in that it contributes to that part of the discourse which says that being female ought to be all about owning clothes, being interested in clothes, wanting to be looked at for the clothes being worn.

Nor should it be assumed that the language of the discourse is used only by men. It is perfectly possible to hear a woman calling another woman a bitch. Women inhabit the same discourse as men, they perpetuate the language, they operate within the same ideology. The discourse creates ways of women thinking about themselves as much as ways of others thinking about women and femaleness. It is true that women are defined as people-oriented and 'sympathetic', within the discourse. It does seem that women use conversation and devices of speech towards social and co-operative ends (where men's talk is often about competing and dominating). But this is unhelpful to sexual equality when such qualities and such talk are ultimately not valued through the power structure of our culture.

References

Argyle M (1992) *The psychology of everyday life* Routledge

Borisoff D & Merrill L (1991)*Listening in everyday life* University of America Press

Hargie O, Saunders C & Dickson D (1994) *Social skills in interpersonal communication* Routledge

Hill C & Stull DE (1987) in V Derlega & J Berg eds *Self-disclosure: theory, research and therapy* Plenum Press

Miller C & Swift K (1979) *Words and women* Penguin

Spender D (1981) *Man made language* Routledge & Kegan Paul

5. Language and Subcultures: Anti-language

Martin Montgomery

Anti-language

Anti-languages may be understood as extreme versions of social dialects. They tend to arise among subcultures and groups that occupy a marginal or precarious position in society, especially where central activities of the group place them outside the law. Often the subculture or group (the 'anti-society') has an antagonistic relationship with society at large and their natural suspicion of outsiders makes it difficult to study their language; but some examples have been documented − notably the language of Polish prison life *(grypserka)* and that of the Calcutta underworld. In addition to these relatively contemporary cases, some historical records survive of a variety known as 'pelting speech' − an argot employed by roving bands of vagabonds in Elizabethan England.

Linguistic features of an anti-language

Anti-languages are basically created by a process of *relexicalization* − the substitution of new words for old. The grammar of the parent language may be preserved, but a distinctive vocabulary develops, particularly − but not solely − in activities and areas that are central to the subculture and that help to set it off most sharply from the established society. Accounts of 'pelting speech', for example, contain over twenty terms for the classes of vagabond including 'rogue', 'wild rogue', 'prigger of prancers' (horse thief), 'counterfeit crank', 'bawdy basket' and so on. Similarly, the language of the Calcutta underworld contains over forty words for the police and over twenty words for bomb.

Making up new words is continuous within the anti-language (another factor that makes them difficult to document − they very quickly go out of date); but often very simple strategies underlie the relexicalization process. An argot in use among bar girls in Addis Ababa included many items formed by regularly substituting /ay/ in place of the first vowel of the original and inserting /er/ before repetition of the final consonant. Thus:

sim ('name')	becomes	saymerm
birr ('dollar')	becomes	bayrerr
heda ('go')	becomes	hayderd
badda ('copulate')	becomes	bayderd

(Demisse & Bender, 1983)

Other forms of innovation include using items from the parent language in metaphorical ways and borrowing items from non-native languages...

37

To some extent, the innovations in vocabulary and the proliferation of terms in certain key areas make possible finer distinctions in meaning than are found necessary in the parent language. It is also the case, however, that some of the new items are actually synonymous with each other and virtually interchangeable. In this respect therefore it is not just relexicalization (same grammar, different vocabulary) that is at work, but a process of *over*-lexicalization, particularly in certain key areas. This has two main consequences: it enhances the possibility for verbal play and display within the anti-society; and it makes the anti-language especially impenetrable to outsiders. The sense of solidarity between members of the subculture is heightened and maintained; and their frequently illicit dealings can remain semi-confidential, even when conducted in relatively public places such as the club, bar or street.

CB radio slang as anti-language

The broad slang at one time used for Citizens' Band (CB) radio transmission has some similarities with an anti-language. In a glossary published around the time of the legalization of CB in Britain there are clearly certain areas of experience which are heavily lexicalized in metaphoric ways. In addition to a vast array of terms concerned with handling the transmission, its quality and the type of rig involved, also listed were several items for 'police', many interchangeable, including 'bear', and 'smokey'. As extensions of such expressions there were several for police-related objects and activities, typified by the following:

police station	'bear cage', 'bear cave'
police helicopter	'bear in the air'
police using radar	'smokey with a camera'
	'portrait painter'
	'kojak with a kodak'
police car	'smokey on rubber'
	'jam sandwich'
	'bubble-gum machine'

When a police vehicle is using flashing lights and a siren, it is 'advertising'. When attempting to be inconspicuous it is 'sitting under the leaves'. Many expressions existed for diverse types of vehicle, including:

lorry without trailer	'bobtail'
flat-fronted lorry	'cabover'
ambulance	'blood wagon', 'meat wagon'
breakdown truck	'dragging wagon' ...

The particular way in which expressions proliferate along metaphorical pathways (e.g. bear → mama bear → lady bear → bear in the air → bear cave → feed the bears; and blood wagon → meat wagon → dragging wagon) is reminiscent of, for instance, Elizabethan pelting speech, in which similar strings of items occur, e.g.:

teeth	'crashing-cheats'
nose	'smelling-cheat'
apron	'belly-cheat'
	(where 'cheat' means 'thing-to-do-with').

Often the particular vocabulary of an anti-language and the metaphorical links within it embody and suggest a distinctive world-view for its users. In the case of CB slang it had distinctly masculine overtones and otherwise it was as if the users were on a trip through a National Park which slides into the fairy tale of the Three Bears...

Anti-language and social structure

In more extreme and hard-edged cases of anti-language, the anti-society that provides the conditions for its generation tends to be much more marginalized and at the same time both more insulated from the wider society and under greater pressure to conform to its norms. The 'second life' of Polish prisons, for example, involves an elaborate caste system of 'people' and 'suckers' which is partially constituted by reference to type of offence, length of stay, and so on, but also in part by the degree of facility displayed by members of the anti-society in their anti-language – *grypserka*. Movement within the hierarchy is dependent on adhering to the rules of an elaborate game in which *grypserka* plays a crucial role. One of the ways in which an inmate can be downgraded to the level of 'sucker' in the social hierarchy is by breaking the rules of verbal contest and another is by selling the secret language to the police. Under conditions such as these, the view of the world constructed in and by the anti-language is much more likely to be totally oppositional in character and its role in determining the speaker's place within the anti-society much more crucial.

On balance, therefore, the language of CB transmission – even before legalization – probably did not constitute an anti-language in the fullest sense of the term. Applying the notion of anti-language to such a variety, however, does help to highlight some of its more salient features. Indeed it is in precisely this kind of exercise that the usefulness of the term lies: not as an absolute category to which particular varieties must conform on an all-or-nothing basis, but as an idea to which given instances approximate more or less closely.

The idea of an anti-language can, perhaps, cast some light on the complicated social significance of 'talking Black' in the British speech community. Linguistically, Black English has identifiable origins in Caribbean (principally Jamaican) Creole. But in the British context its precise point of geographical origin is not immediately at issue. As far as is known to date, Patois in Britain does not vary much from region to region. On the contrary it belongs not so much to a locality but to a particular, ethnically defined social group. At the simplest level, close integration with the Black community entails the frequent use of Patois and the consequent likelihood of a high degree of competence in it. But this fact of use based on networks of particular kinds of relationship can take on a larger social significance. In 'Black' settings its use conveys solidarity between speakers. It is the easiest way to be on the same wavelength. But in 'White' or mixed settings use of Patois inevitably comes to symbolize social distance from mainstream society and to count as an assertion of ethnic identity. Its significance in this respect is all the more marked if as a variety it is perceived as very distinct from local English norms. The more linguistically distinct it sounds, the more it can come to symbolize social distance. From this perspective the African traces in Patois – in voice-set and intonation in particular – can clearly play a crucial role: so that, for at least some Black speakers some of the time in some situations, 'talking Black' can provide a mode of resistance on the linguistic level to the dominant social order. In its potential for articulating a form of symbolic resistance Patois has some resemblance to anti-language.

Anti-language and the speech community

The notion of an anti-language, therefore, can be used to illuminate certain kinds of social dialect. It can also be used, however, to clarify the notion of speech community. It is not just that a speech community is likely to embrace and include a range of different forms of speech. Nor is it just a question of these differing forms of speech all being linguistically equal and equivalent. Nor even is it a question of a speech community consistently attaching a higher value to some varieties over others, despite their linguistic equality. In the final analysis, viewed from the perspective of anti-language, the speech community emerges as an arena of competing affiliations and antagonistic differences.

Reference

Demisse T & Bender ML (1983) 'An argot of Addis Ababa unattached girls' *Language and Society* 12: pp339–347

6. **With an 'Uh Uh' Here and a
Mutter There**

Wendy Wallace

It's good to talk, says Bob Hoskins in the BT ad which eggs on middle-class university students to call home. But the language of grown-ups alienates other teenagers who live in a culture where it's cool to be silent and surly... Communication skills could empower these disadvantaged young people.

Sixteen-year-old Shauna Rose, smart and streetwise with orange tips in her carefully straightened black hair, was ejected from school and her Year 12 course in health and social care in September last year. It was the second day of term. She is bitter. 'I came home from Jamaica just to do it,' she says. 'I went and bought all the pencils and pens. But they don't listen to you in that school. Once you have a fight, they don't want to know.'

Shauna Rose, well-known after five eventful years, was asked to leave because of her attitude to teachers. What did she say, when she was called into the head's office for the interview which resulted in her expulsion? 'I didn't say nuttin. They just want you to hear their side.'

Young people like Shauna Rose, who regularly face tricky encounters – whether with headteachers, probation officers, the police or other officials – are those least likely to have the skills to put their position across, according to a new survey on communication in teenage years by the Trust for the Study of Adolescence.

With money from BT, researcher Dr Liza Catan and her colleagues mapped the communication patterns of more than 4,000 teenagers around the country. Teachers emerged well: only 11 per cent of the teenagers interviewed rated their communication with teachers as poor.

But while most reported broadly positive feelings about communication in and outside their families, socially or materially disadvantaged teenagers had the highest levels of contact with professionals, particularly those who deal with offending, benefits and social care. One homeless young man, having been given a bureaucratic runaround which would challenge the most articulate and authoritative adult, in the end simply said to the DSS officer 'You just take the piss' – and walked out, still hungry and with the benefits claim unresolved.

Dr Catan says the ability to stand back in such situations, to reflect on what is needed to make communication work, and to have the skills to make it work, would empower disadvantaged teenagers. Arguably, these young people would then be less at risk of finding themselves homeless and friendless.

But for people working with vulnerable teenagers, improving communication is central. Martin Kenward is head of an East Sussex unit for excluded pupils. Part of his job is to go into schools and negotiate on pupils' behalf, where relationships have broken down. 'If there is a difficulty,' he says, 'some teachers find it hard to get the discussion down to a human being level. A well-educated parent can intervene, but if the child is on his or her own and has weak skills, it's a very big problem.' Some pupils in his Eastbourne tutorial unit may appear brashly confident with their friends, but are ill-equipped to deal with the age of multimedia. 'They cringe, some of them, if we try to get them to use the telephone,' he says, 'and when asked to ring up employers they crumple completely. We get them to practise talking to us on the internal phone systems.'

But it is not only children in special units who can lack fluency in English as it is spoken in the world of teachers and employers. John Fullman is head of English at Southfields Community College in south London. He says the pupils are mainly from working-class backgrounds and the school culture is one of inarticulacy. 'There's a cachet in being inarticulate. In answering uh?, from the back of the throat to questions,' he says. 'The kids with received pronunciation accents are sneered at because you can't be tough and RP.' But Mr. Fullman says his pupils are, for the most part, able to fit the mode of communication to the context.

Most could, he believes, summon a more formal and explicit vocabulary when necessary. 'The ones who can't adjust for the audience are the ones who aren't going to get on,' he says. 'The same ones who can never learn French are the ones who can never make the transition from south London to standard English. Even those aren't necessarily bad communicators. Just narrow.'

Dr Catan says that teachers need to be mindful of pupils' need to communicate beyond the classroom. 'The question is not: can they communicate?', she says. 'But can they communicate in the ways required to get them well educated, trained and, eventually, employed?' 'Proponents of "youth culture" do young people from less advantaged backgrounds no favours by leading them to believe they can do fine without learning "adult" communication rules.'

Young women, the researchers note, find talking easier than young men. 'Girls were more positive about communication, communicated more often and with a wider range of people than their male peers,' says Liza Catan. This gender difference transcends class ones. 'Many parents of teenage boys will mention the zombie phase,' she says. 'I used to tease my own sons when all they did was grunt at each other. Girls often have a kind of chatterbox poise at that stage that boys completely lack.'...

Tricia Kreitman, psychologist and agony aunt on *Mizz* magazine, says that not communicating is one of the most powerful statements teenagers have available to them. 'A lot of young people feel totally disempowered in schools. Or they have problems at home and feel that adults there don't listen to them. They can feel talking is pointless, and it gives them great power not to communicate with people who want them to.'...

However, the survey provided little ammunition for any generalised statement that teenagers communicated less well then they used to. 'A lot astounded us with the degree of their fluency and articulateness,' says Dr Catan. 'You can't say that teenagers don't communicate effectively. But important groups don't.' Part of the purpose of the research is to design interventions to help vulnerable young people communicate better.

But, according to Roz Brody of the Trust, it may be necessary to target those around teenagers. 'As I'm talking to young people, I'm getting more concerned about adults' communication,' she says. 'It seems sometimes as if young people are communicating quite well but adults aren't listening.'

Reference

Getting through: effective communication in the teenage years The BT Forum: Tel 0800 800 926

7. Language, Hearing and Speech

Oliver Sacks

I first became interested in the deaf — their history, their predicament, their language, their culture — when I was sent Harlan Lane's books to review. In particular, I was haunted by descriptions of isolated deaf people who had failed to acquire any language whatever: their evident intellectual disabilities and, equally seriously, the mishaps in emotional and social development to which they might fall prey in the absence of any authentic language or communication. What is necessary, I wondered, for us to become complete human beings? Is our humanity, so-called, partly dependent on language? What happens to us if we fail to acquire any language? Does language develop spontaneously and naturally, or does it require contact with other human beings?

One way — a dramatic way — of exploring these topics is to look at human beings deprived of language; and deprivation of language, in the form of aphasia, has been a central preoccupation of neurologists since the 1860s... But aphasia is the deprivation of language (through a stroke or other cerebral accident) in an already formed mind, a completed individual. One might say that language has already done its work here (if it has work to do) in the formation of mind and character. If one is to explore the fundamental role of language, one needs to study not its loss after being developed, but its failure to develop.

And yet I found it difficult to imagine such things: I had patients who had lost language, patients with aphasia, but could not imagine what it might be like not to have acquired language to begin with.

Two years ago, at the Braefield School for the Deaf, I met Joseph, a boy of eleven who had just entered school for the first time — an eleven-year-old with no language whatever. He had been born deaf, but this had not been realised until he was in his fourth year. His failure to talk, or understand speech, at the normal age was put down to 'retardation', then to 'autism', and these diagnoses had clung to him. When his deafness finally became apparent he was seen as 'deaf and dumb', dumb not only literally, but metaphorically, and there was never any real attempt to teach him language.

Joseph longed to communicate, but could not. Neither speaking nor writing nor signing was available to him, only gesture and pantomime, and a marked ability to draw. What has happened to him? I kept asking myself. What is going on inside, how has he come to such a pass? He looked alive and animated, but profoundly baffled: his eyes were attracted to speaking mouths and signing hands — they darted to our mouths and hands, inquisitively, uncomprehendingly, and, it seemed to me, yearningly. He perceived that something was 'going on' between us, but he could not comprehend what it was — he had, as yet, almost no idea of symbolic communication, of what it was to have a symbolic currency, to exchange meaning.

Previously deprived of opportunity – for he had never been exposed to Sign – and undermined in motive and affect (above all, the joy that play and language should give), Joseph was now just beginning to pick up a little Sign, beginning to have some communication with others. This, manifestly, gave him great joy; he wanted to stay at school all day, all night, all weekend, all the time. His distress at leaving school was painful to see, for going home meant, for him, return to the silence, return to a hopeless communicational vacuum, where he could have no converse, no commerce, with his parents, neighbours, friends; it meant being overlooked, becoming a nonperson, again.

This was very poignant, extraordinary – without any exact parallel in my experience. I was partly reminded of a two-year-old infant trembling on the verge of language – but Joseph was eleven, was like an eleven-year-old in most other ways. I was partly reminded in a way of a non-verbal animal, but no animal ever gave the feeling of yearning for language as Joseph did. Hughlings-Jackson, it came to me, once compared aphasics to dogs – but dogs seem complete and contented in their languagelessness, whereas the aphasic has a tormenting sense of loss. And Joseph, too: he clearly had an anguished sense of something missing, a sense of his own crippledness and deficit. He made me think of wild children, feral children, though clearly he was not 'wild' but a creature of our civilisation and habits – but one who was nonetheless radically cut-off.

Joseph was unable, for example, to communicate how he had spent the weekend – one could not really ask him, even in Sign: he could not even grasp the *idea* of a question, much less formulate an answer. It was not only language that was missing: there was not, it was evident, a clear sense of the past, of 'a day ago' as distinct from 'a year ago'. There was a strange lack of historical sense, the feeling of a life that lacked autobiographical and historical dimensions, the feeling of a life that only existed in the moment, in the present.

His visual intelligence – his ability to solve visual puzzles and problems – was good, in radical contrast to his profound difficulties with verbally based problems. He could draw and liked drawing: he did good diagrams of the room, he enjoyed drawing people; he 'got' cartoons, he 'got' visual concepts. It was this that above all gave me the feeling of intelligence, but an intelligence largely confined to the visual. He 'picked up' tic-tac-toe and was soon very good at it; I had the sense that he might readily learn checkers or chess.

Joseph saw, distinguished, categorised, used; he had no problems with *perceptual* categorisation or generalisation, but he could not, it seemed, go much beyond this, hold abstract ideas in mind, reflect, play, plan. He seemed completely literal – unable to juggle images or hypotheses or possibilities, unable to enter an imaginative or figurative realm. And yet, one still felt, he was of normal intelligence, despite these manifest limitations of intellectual functioning. It was not that he lacked a mind, but that he was not *using his mind fully.*

It is clear that thought and language have quite separate (biological) origins, that the world is examined and mapped and responded to long before the advent of language, that there is a huge range of thinking – in animals, or infants – long before the emergence of language. (No one has examined this more beautifully than Piaget, but it is obvious to every parent – or pet lover.) A human being is not mindless or mentally deficient without language, but he is severely restricted in the range of his thoughts, confined, in effect, to an immediate, small world.

For Joseph, the beginnings of a communication, a language, had now started, and he was tremendously excited at this. The school had found that it was not just formal instruction that he needed, but playing with language, language games, as with a toddler learning language for the first time. In this, it was hoped, he might begin to acquire language and conceptual thinking, to acquire it in the *act* of intellectual play. I found myself thinking of the twins Luria described, who had been in a sense so 'retarded' because their language was so bad, and how they improved, immeasurably, when they acquired it. Would this too be possible for Joseph?...

Though a well-developed, active, bright eleven-year-old, Joseph was in this sense still an infant – denied the power, the world, that language opens up. In Joseph Church's words:

> *Language opens up new orientations and new possibilities for learning and for action, dominating and transforming pre-verbal experiences... Language is not just one function among many... but an all-pervasive characteristic of the individual such that he [sic] becomes a* verbal organism *(all of whose experiences and actions and conceptions are now altered in accordance with a verbalised or symbolic experience).*

> *Language transforms experience... Through language one can induct the child into a purely symbolic realm of past and future, of remote places, of ideal relationships, of hypothetical events, of imaginative literature, of imaginary entities ranging from werewolves to pi-mesons...*

> *At the same time the learning of language transforms the individual in such a way that he is enabled to do new things for himself, or to do old things in new ways. Language permits us to deal with things at a distance, to act on them without physically handling them. First, we can act on other people, or on objects through people... Second, we can manipulate symbols in ways impossible with the things they stand for, and so arrive at novel and even creative versions of reality... We can verbally rearrange situations which in themselves would resist rearrangement ... we can isolate features which in fact cannot be isolated ... we can juxtapose objects and events far separated in time and space ... we can, if we will, turn the universe symbolically inside out.*

We can do this, but Joseph could not. Joseph could not reach that symbolic plane which is the normal human birthright from earliest childhood on. He seemed, like an animal, or an infant, to be stuck in the present, to be confined to literal and immediate perception, though made aware of this by a consciousness that no infant could have...

47

None of us can remember how we 'acquired' language... Nor are we, as parents, called on to 'teach' our children language; they acquire it, or seem to, in the most automatic way, through virtue of being children, our children, and the communicative exchanges between us.

It is customary to distinguish grammar, verbal meanings, and communicative intent – the syntax, the semantics, the pragmatics of language – but as Bruner and others remind us, these always go together in the learning and use of language; and therefore it is not language but language *use* we must study. The *first* language use, the first communication, is usually between mother and child, and language is acquired, arises, *between* the two.

One is born with one's senses; these are 'natural'. One can develop motor skills, naturally, by oneself. But one cannot acquire language by oneself: *this* skill comes in a unique category. It is impossible to acquire language without some essential innate ability, but this ability is only activated by another person who already possesses linguistic power and competence. It is only through transaction (or, as Vygotsky would say, 'negotiation') with another that the language is achieved. (Wittgenstein writes in general terms of the 'language games we must all learn to play', and Brown speaks of 'the original word game' played by mother and child.)

The mother – or father, or teacher, or indeed anyone who talks with the child – leads the infant step by step to higher levels of language; she leads him into language, and into the world picture it embodies *(her* world-picture, because it is her language; and beyond this, the world-picture of the culture she belongs to). The mother must always be a step ahead, in what Vygotsky calls the 'zone of proximal development'; the infant cannot move into, or conceive of, the next stage ahead except through its being occupied and communicated to him by his mother.

But the mother's words, and the world behind them, would have no sense for the infant unless they corresponded to something in his own experience. He has an independent experience of the world given to him by his senses, and it is this which forms a correlation or confirmation of the mother's language, and in turn, is given meaning by it. It is the mother's language, internalised by the child, that allows it to move from sensation into 'sense', to ascend from a perceptual into a conceptual world.

Social and emotional intercourse, intellectual intercourse too, starts from the first day of life. Vygotsky was greatly interested in these prelinguistic, preintellectual stages of life, but his especial interest was in language and thought and how they come together in the development of the child. Vygotsky never forgets that language is always, and at once, both social and intellectual in function, nor does he forget for a moment the relation of intellect and affect, of how all communication, all thought, is also emotional, reflecting 'the personal needs and interests, the inclinations and impulses' of the individual.

The corollary to all this is that if communication goes awry, it will affect intellectual growth, social intercourse, language development, and emotional attitudes, all at once, simultaneously and inseparably. And this, of course, is what may happen; what does happen, all too frequently, when a child is born deaf...

Poor dialogue, communicative defeat, ... leads not only to intellectual constriction but to timidity and passivity; creative dialogue, a rich communicative interchange in childhood, awakens the imagination and mind, leads to a self-sufficiency, a boldness, a playfulness, a humour, that will be with the person for the rest of his life.

...I went to visit [six-year-old] Charlotte and her family [in Albany]; the first thing that struck me was that they *were* a family – full of fun, full of liveliness, full of questions, all together. There was none of the isolation one so often sees with the deaf – and none of the 'primitive' language ('What's this? What's that? Do this! Do that!')... Charlotte herself was full of questions, full of curiosity, full of life – a delightful, imaginative, and playful child, vividly turned to the world and to others. She was disappointed that I did not sign, but instantly commandeered her parents as interpreters and questioned me closely about the wonders of New York.

About thirty miles from Albany is a forest and river, and here I later drove with Charlotte, her parents, and her brother. Charlotte loves the natural world as much as the human world, but loves it in an intelligent way. She had an eye for different habitats, for the way things live together; she perceived co-operation and competition, the dynamics of existence. She was fascinated by the ferns that grew by the river, saw that they were very different from the flowers, understood the distinction between spores and seeds. She would exclaim excitedly in Sign over all the shapes and colours, but then attend and pause to ask, 'How?', and 'Why?', and 'What if?' Clearly, it was not isolated facts that she wanted, but connections, understanding, a world with sense and meaning. Nothing showed me more clearly the passage from a perceptual to a conceptual world, a passage impossible without complex dialogue – a dialogue that first occurs with the parents, but is then internalized as 'talking to oneself,' as thought.

Dialogue launches language, the mind, but once it is launched we develop a new power, 'inner speech', and it is this that is indispensable for our further development, our thinking. 'Inner speech,' says Vygotsky, 'is speech almost without words ... it is not the interior aspect of external speech, it is a function in itself... While in external speech thought is embodied in words, in inner speech words die as they bring forth thought. Inner speech is to a large extent thinking in pure meanings.' We start with dialogue, with language that is external and social, but then to think, to become ourselves, we have to move to a monologue, to inner speech. Inner speech is essentially solitary, and it is profoundly mysterious, as unknown to science, Vygotsky writes, as 'the other side of the moon.' 'We are our language', it is often said; but our real language, our real identity, lies in inner speech, in that ceaseless stream and generation of meaning that constitutes the individual mind. It is through inner speech that the child develops his own concepts and meanings; it is through inner speech that he achieves his own identity; it is through inner speech, finally, that he constructs his own world. And the inner speech (or inner Sign) of the deaf may be very distinctive.

It is evident to her parents that Charlotte constructs her world in a different way, perhaps radically so: that she employs predominantly visual thought patterns, and that she 'thinks differently' about physical objects. I was struck by the graphic quality, the fullness of her descriptions. Her parents spoke too of this fullness: 'All the characters or creatures or objects Charlotte talks about are *placed*', her mother said; 'spatial reference is essential to ASL [American Sign Language]. When Charlotte signs, the whole scene is set up; you can see where everyone or everything is; it is all visualised with a detail that would be rare for the hearing.' This placing of objects and people in specific locations, this use of elaborate, spatial reference had been striking in Charlotte, her parents said, since the age of four and a half – already at that age she had gone beyond them, shown a sort of 'staging' power, an 'architectural' power that they had seen in other deaf people – but rarely in the hearing.

Language and thought, for us, are always personal – our utterances express ourselves, as does our inner speech. Language often feels to us, therefore, like an effusion, a sort of spontaneous transmission of self. It does not occur to us at first that it must have a *structure*, a structure of an immensely intricate and formal kind. We are unconscious of this structure; we do not see it, any more than we see the tissues, the organs, the architectural make-up of our own bodies. But the enormous, unique freedom of language would not be possible without the most extreme grammatical constraints. It is grammar, first of all, that makes a language possible, that allows us to articulate our thoughts, our selves, in utterance.

References

Brown R (1958) *Words and things* The Free Press

Bruner J (1983) *Child's talk: learning to use language* Oxford University Press

Church J (1961) *Language and the discovery of reality* Random House

Hughlings-Jackson J (1915) 'Hughlings-Jackson on aphasia and kindred affections of speech, together with a complete bibliography of his publications on speech and a reprint of some of the more important papers' *Brain* xxxviii: pp1–190

Luria AR & Yudovich FI (1958) *Speech and the development of mental processes in the child* Staples Press

Vygotsky LS (1962) *Thought and language* ed and trans by Eugenia Hanfmann & Gertrude Vahar, MIT Press and John Wiley & Sons

Language, Communication and the Teacher

An inescapable human characteristic is our idiosyncratic repertoire of language and communication skills, made up of the words that we use, the way we apply them, the structure we devise in order to build utterances with them, and to which we add nods ands shrugs, grunts and smiles, gestures and physical contact. We acquire and refine these skills as we mature, usually without any conscious effort. They are part of our identity, but not one that we are often aware of controlling as we do, for example, our physical appearance. That is quite odd, because both what we say and what we look like have the same function in our experience. They are the clues about ourselves that we communicate to the world and which others interpret — in one way or another.

What goes on in classroom interactions and in other academic contexts is not typical of human communication in general. One of the characteristics is constant 'noise'; another is the use of questions and explanations. The classroom has noise in common with television programmes or debates in parliament; questions and explanations are typical of interactions such as those we have with solicitors, officials in the civil service, or prospective employers. Ordinary conversation, by contrast, has lapses into silence, and everyday situations such as shopping or being on a bus consist principally of non-verbal communication, punctuated by the communication of transaction. There are a few professional contexts which do make use of silence, and these are often characterised by a reflection on something, perhaps a problem or an aspect of behaviour. An example of this type of communication might be a session with a therapist or a social worker.

As teachers, we are engaged in developing and changing learners' skills, knowledge and attitudes. This is a nurturing, contemplative activity surely, using the capabilities of the facilitator rather than those of the manager. Teachers have responsibility for more than just the quality of their performance. We have to meet the intellectual and personal needs of individuals, interpret and present our subject in a meaningful way, and manage the learning environment. In order to achieve proficiency in teaching we must be watchful of all aspects of our communication, including taking responsibility for the correct understanding of meaning and being aware of the controlling function of language. This is not something humans are able to do easily without practice.

Might it be that we do not often review the habits of our own language use because to do so is difficult and to adapt our communication style and strategy even more so? It could be argued that the easiest aspect of changing communication is developing new characteristics; this is something we habitually ask students to do and if there is a convincing case for change they achieve it very effectively. So, new vocabulary is acquired as new concepts are explored. But we must not take this for granted.

Experience of the world erects barriers to effective communication and learning. Personal value systems – ours and our students' – can lead to misunderstandings between us. It is our responsibility to know enough about the processes of human interaction to be aware of this and to be able to take action to counter it. The idiosyncratic way academics use language may be absorbed subconsciously but is more likely to become a communication skill which the student can manipulate after analysis and reflection, in which the teacher may have been a guide.

8.   Making Language Work

Martin Powell & Jonathan Solity

Language has enormous power to permit each of us to reconstruct reality, or fantasy, to depict history from a time before people, to imagine the future, to plan, to describe, to communicate our innermost feelings and thoughts, and to examine the very nature of language itself...

Our interest in language, however, extends beyond its obvious involvement in the processes of influence. Language is not just the oil that lubricates the cogs of social interaction and private thought. It is not neutral, not an impartial device for communicating and thinking. It is, in our view, locked into these processes themselves. Choosing words, consciously or otherwise, is neither an accidental, nor an incidental, part of communicating.

Language in teaching

Education is about communicating, about influencing the development of people, about shaping the ideas and the behaviour of future generations by the previous generations. Education relies heavily on language, not only as an integral part of the teaching process, but also as a means of controlling the content, methods, and values conveyed in that process. Since communicating is the very stuff of teaching and education, the use of language in that sphere is of specific interest to us and deserves close scrutiny.

Suppose that you are required to teach some aspect of engineering or cookery. If you reflect for a moment, you will recognise what sort of an activity this is. You are required to transmit some part of your culture, something that you know, to others. Apart from focusing on the engineering task or the cookery task itself in your preparation for the lesson, you will also need to teach the language of engineering or cookery, as far as these are necessary for the particular item to be taught. You might need to describe, for example, the process of basting and the use of a basting spoon, or describe a flange and its purpose in the particular machine assembly that you are examining. There is thus a technical language component to what the student must learn.

The next component of language in this teaching process is the language of instruction. Apart from the technical and specialised vocabulary of engineering or cookery, you will use language which is specific to the teaching situation. The phrases that you use will mark the fact that you are the teacher and the students are learners, for example:

> 'I want you to look very closely at this part'

> 'Now, can anyone tell me why it is that...'

These phrases are unusual phrases, not the substance of everyday communication, but they are conventional, in the sense that the students expect you to talk like that when you are in the teaching mode. If you try this style as, say, a parent, you are likely to occasion groans and the glazing over of eyes that parents get when they try deliberately to adopt a didactic role with their children. In the workshop, in the home economics room, in the classroom, there is an acceptance of the instructional language mode. The tone of voice, the directness of questions and of instructions, and the proportion of the interaction taken by you as the teacher will be acceptable in this context. Teachers are sometimes accused of continuing these aspects of language into other social settings, a source of annoyance or amusement to others, but then the same charge might be levelled at other workers, who take a mode of language away from the workplace into other contexts.

As a teacher of engineering or cookery, you have to use the technical language of your subject and the language of teaching or instruction. The language of instruction will reflect speech that is used commonly by all teachers and which reflects a particular teaching style. However, a cookery teacher or a CDT teacher might also use a style common to teachers who have to manage practical subjects, where, for example, dangers are present and so routines are necessary. The language of explaining about lighting a gas jet or a blow-torch might be considerably more directive than the language of considering the origins of the First World War.

Much of the language that you use in the teaching situation is, none the less, your individual language. This is your language of interpersonal style. It will change from situation to situation, but there is a consistency which represents you. Unless you are capable of putting on a complete act, your interpersonal style is your own and is present in every social situation in which you take part. The language you use conveys a great deal of information to those with whom you engage in conversation.

Personal language style

Let us consider some of the information that your personal language conveys to others. In so doing, let us also suppose that the following process is involved in your interaction with another person:

- What you mean to say
- How you manage to say what you mean
- What the other person thinks you will say
- What the other person thinks you said
- What the other person thinks you meant

In commenting on this process, we are also making lots of guesses as to what is going on, and so when we talk about looking at the information that your personal language conveys we ought to remind ourselves that we are making an interpretation too.

One of the authors recalls watching a group of children working with their teacher on recording the colour of cars owned by the families of the children. The results had been displayed on a bar chart. The teacher asked the children to think of questions that they could ask about the chart. The first two respondents asked questions of the 'how many' variety – 'how many families had brown cars?' The third respondent asked a different question – 'why did so many families buy red or white or silver cars?' 'Oh!' laughed the teacher, 'that's not something we can work out from the chart. Has anyone else got another question?' The third child looked a little embarrassed, aware that, somehow, he'd missed the point. In fact, the teacher probably had not realised that her request to the class was more open-ended than she had intended. The child had not read what was in the teacher's mind. The result was that the child had entered fully into the spirit of enquiry, but had not asked a numerical question. Nevertheless, he learned a very important lesson about life. Adults have the power to move the goal posts.

Another point that needs to be made is that language can convey information over and above that which is conveyed by the content. How you talk is part of your self-presentation, part of the data on which others attempt to predict you, and on which they can base their interaction with you. (In addition, of course, there are non-verbal factors, such as your clothes, your movements, your facial expression, that are all part of the way that you are 'interpreted' by others. Some of the accounts of classroom management, for example, have recognised the importance of some of the non-verbal signals in helping teachers assume status and control among groups of students.)

Your accent, your use of certain phrases and vocabulary, your voice tone, your use of pauses, your speech hesitations, will all combine to convey your relative status. People with whom you converse may draw inferences about the group or subgroup to which you belong. They will judge how you feel about the situation, whether you are confident or hesitant, on top of the job or struggling, interested or bored, involved or detached. They will make judgements about whether you are easy to approach, whether you like them, whether you are enjoying yourself, whether you are predictable.

All of these processes will be in operation as well as the actual content of your lesson. Apart from what you *mean* to convey about the matter in hand, there will be all these other signals available to be interpreted. There may be aspects, as well, that arise from the agendas of your students, which influence how they view and interpret the situation...

These influences, that impinge on the student, may affect what the student understands of your lesson. They may affect how the student sees you or responds to the interaction. In whatever ways you seek to control the language and your own self-presentation, the meaning that is abstracted from the interaction depends, in part, on the interpretation from the other person. This does not absolve us, however, from having a direct responsibility for the way in which we use language. Language conveys so much of what we think, not only about the topic of conversation but also about the person with whom we are talking, that it would be naïve to pay no regard to its influence.

We shall argue at a later point that communication, by its very nature, is liable to engender misinterpretations and that to disregard the likelihood of this happening is to contribute to interpersonal tension and conflict.

Straight and crooked talking

There are, of course, people who make a living out of paying attention to language by polishing up the way that their clients present themselves. Elocution is available for those who feel that their speech affects adversely their social or professional development. It may be that there is a specific problem about the way in which you present that obscures what you mean. To deal with such an obstacle is, no doubt, sensible.

There are, however, other practitioners of the art of communication whose business is concerned less with making accessible what their clients wish to say, and more with developing wider powers of influence over audiences. One of our interests in this chapter is to look at aspects of language that obscure meaning, to bring those aspects forward for consideration, and to emphasise throughout that, for each of us, the moral position is to strive for understanding, not to use language to manipulate or deceive. Our emphasis on paying attention to the language of interaction is towards a greater understanding of interpersonal processes. Language can be used for effect. Politicians and other public speakers employ language devices in their speech that enhance the emphasis of what they want to say and that win greater acceptance from their audience.

This has been strikingly illustrated by both Atkinson (1984) and Heritage & Greatbach (1986). They have drawn attention to specific techniques used by politicians to earn applause during their speeches. One of the most effective relates to the use of inversions. A much quoted example is President Kennedy's request to Americans in the 1960s: 'Ask not what your country can do for you but what you can do for your country.' During the 1987 UK general election campaign, Neil Kinnock, leader of the Labour Party, declared, 'I will die for my country, but I will not let my country die for me'. A more notorious example, from one of Hollywood's wittiest women, Mae West, was, 'It's not the men in my life that matters, but the life in my men.'

Apart from the influence over audiences that can be achieved by the manipulation of the form of one's sentences, there are many ways in which illegitimate influence can be gained by arguments themselves. Robert Thouless (1974) wrote a book entitled *Straight and Crooked Thinking* in 1930, which remains a classic in describing illegitimate argument. In the appendix of that book, Thouless lists thirty-eight dishonest tricks of argument together with his suggestions for dealing with them. For example, his fourth point is referred to as extension of an opponent's proposition by contradiction or misrepresentation of it (p193).

In the body of the text, Thouless explains how, in the course of a discussion, it is possible for one person (A) to take an extreme position. The second person (B) might win the argument by remaining reasonable. However, if B is persuaded to respond in kind by countering the wild claims by equally wild claims, then A can score by simply attacking the first insupportable wild claim made by B. For example, let us suppose the following conversation occurs:

(A)   'What with all these modern approaches in education, no wonder standards are falling!'

(B)   'I don't think that is true.'

(A)   'Discipline is non-existent and more and more children are leaving school totally illiterate because of these child-centred approaches.'

(B)   'That's rubbish! Standards are rising.'

(A)   'If that's the case, how do you explain the report from HMI on literacy standards on young people entering the Employment Training scheme?'

This short fictitious exchange suffices to illustrate that B was drawn into making sweeping generalisations and was left exposed. It also illustrates another dishonest trick described by Thouless as 'proof by selected instances'. In the scenario, A refers to one report as a means of upholding the claim that standards are falling. Interested readers are recommended to read Thouless to supplement this short example.

Manipulative language

Language is not just open to misinterpretation, therefore. It can be deliberately manipulated to exert influence over the way others understand it. An example of this manipulation of language can be found in an advert placed in *The Guardian* newspaper (17 September 1988), in which the Tobacco Advisory Council reproduced three extracts from three other newspapers describing accounts of actual physical aggression towards the police in quite graphic details:

'WPC beaten senseless as 60 cheer'

'Black and blue line: 50 police are beaten up every day of the year'

'Hero Cop Shot. He tackled bank gang'

Then the advert quotes from another newspaper story:

'and to add insult to injury ...

Ban on Police Smokes. Smoking became a criminal offence today as far as some policemen were concerned. They are now banned from lighting up at their stations and in patrol cars.'

The final point made by the Tobacco Advisory Council states:

'After the bricks, bottles and bullets, shouldn't the police be spared the attentions of the anti-smoking lobby?'

By implication, the anti-smoking lobby's views are associated with the decision to end smoking in some sections of the police force. By further implication, the anti-smoking lobby is associated with some of the violence towards the police. One way of reading the final remark is as follows: 'After the bricks, bottles, bullets of the anti-smoking lobby shouldn't the police be spared its attentions?'

We accept that this is merely one interpretation, but the case for leaving poor bobbies to have their smokes in peace is that they have already had to face such harrowing violence. 'If you deplore the violence towards the police you will also deplore this restriction', seems to be the message of the advert. The issue of concern here is not the arguments for and against smoking but whether the association of ideas is a legitimate communication or one which seeks to use undue influence in changing the opinion of others.

Let us leave that example to make a general point. The reader might consider that we are taking a very harsh attitude in ascribing intentionality to the words that are used in communication. Words convey a complexity of meanings which are dependent upon the context and the nature of the discourse, among many factors, in order for any precision to be achieved. Is it reasonable to hold individuals responsible for the interpretations of their words that others place upon them? Is not the receiver also responsible for the interpretation? Might not some people deliberately, or unwittingly, misinterpret the communications of others?

In the example above, where the communication is carefully prepared with a conscious intention of producing an effect upon the reader, it seems not unreasonable to place the onus for the interpretation of the message on the sender. But what about spontaneous conversation between people in the course of their everyday communications? Do we always have to assume single-handed responsibility for the course of the communication, for the effectiveness of the message?

One of the authors recalls how, as a newly qualified teacher, he was drawn into debates, not unwillingly, with the headteacher, who, while seeking discussion on educational issues with someone straight from college, used to get quite heated. On such occasions, he would say, 'You people ... you come in here with your theories...!' More recently, this author heard an item on the radio concerning a commissioned report on the Metropolitan Police Force in which the firm of consultants had drawn attention to a few police officers whose attitude to the public was not acceptable. The spokesman, a senior officer, had commented that 'these people' needed to be identified and evidence acquired in order to be able to proceed properly with their dismissal. By using the terms 'you people' and 'these people', both the headteacher and the police spokesman were seeking to establish a category. For the one, the category might have consisted of 'wet-behind-the-ears-straight-from-college-full-of-ideas-and-no-experience-probationary-teachers'. For the other, the category might have been 'officers-who-let-the-side-down-and-give-the-force-a-bad-name'. The impression that is given in both cases is that there are categories into which it is useful to place individuals and to which you can ascribe attributes belonging to all the people who are included in that category.

Our view is that speakers, and particularly writers, are responsible for the choice of words. If the writer pleads that her or his intention was different from the message as received, then she or he must bear the responsibility for the ambiguity of the message. Speakers are responsible for checking what the hearers understand of their communication, although as we shall mention later, listeners also have a responsibility to check out their understanding.

One further point about language is that it is a basis for thinking. It may be argued that, as well as taking care in their external communication, individuals should be careful with the language that they use to think with, in that if they get into the habit of thinking with language that is careless, overladen with bias, or prejudicial, then it will be much harder to engage in an open discussion with others.

The language of control

The previous section has drawn attention to the ways that language can be used to influence people, in terms of both the style of presentation and the arguments put forward. Let us now turn to some of the ways that language can be used in a variety of situations as a means of control. We begin by looking at the way that language can be a mechanism for controlling culture. Michael Sheridan in *The Independent*, writing about Archbishop Lefebvre of the Catholic Church, described some of the aspects of the archbishop's practice that marked him out as ultra-conservative and in opposition to the main body of the Church:

> *In its place, his followers celebrate the so-called Tridentine Mass codified by Pope Pius V, a solemn and mystical Latin rite. 'The fact that Latin is a dead language,' observes the archbishop, 'is in its favour. It is the best means of protecting the expression of faith against linguistic changes which come about naturally in the course of time.'*
>
> *(The Independent, 30 June 1988)*

Archbishop Lefebvre has a clear idea of the power of language. If you fail to halt its progress, then concepts that can only be enshrined linguistically become eroded, as words that have been used in their description begin to take on new meaning. From this, it can be seen that concepts are inseparable from the language used to express them. This gives rise to a number of linguistic and communicative problems. Not only does the meaning of words change, as the archbishop points out, but also the meaning of words can vary from situation to situation and from individual to individual. And yet it might be that this process of change is all part of human progress and that it mainly poses problems for someone with fixed views rather than for others.

Yet another example of control is to be found in relation to knowledge. The social psychologist, Rom Harré, in a conversation with Miller, makes the following comment:

> *Knowledge is never stationary. There is a kind of seepage. Knowledge is moving through society all the time. If we think of knowledge as socially located, it can start its social journey in highly technical institutions, an esoteric knowledge known only to a few. But soon it begins to leak away and permeate the whole of society.*
>
> (Miller, 1983: 66)

In this extract, Harré is talking not about language as such, but the process of 'seepage' might very well be associated with language. It is probable that the conceptual or scientific advances made within the highly technical institutions are conveyed to others more by language than, for example, by the spy's photographs. This permeation of knowledge through society does pose problems, none the less, and not only for those who want some aspects of the world to stand still. The problem is to do with the use of language as the method of conveying meaning.

Language and the control of meaning

In a conversation with Bryan Magee, John Searle makes the following observation about Wittgenstein's views on meaning:

> *In his later work, he abandoned the picture theory of meaning in favour of a use or tool conception of meaning. He urges us to think of words as tools, think of sentences as instruments. To get a correct conception of language we need simply to look at how it functions in real life, we need to look at what people do with words. He says, 'For a large class of cases – though not for all – in which we employ the word "meaning" it can be defined thus: the meaning of a word is its use in the language'.*

> (Magee, 1987: 326)

If we take this point about the meaning of a word being determined by its use, then Wittgenstein sets us some more problems. In his *Philosophical Investigations*, he writes 'Language is a labyrinth of paths. You approach from *one* side and know your way about; you approach the same place from another side and no longer know your way about'. (Wittgenstein, 1984:203)

Meanings of words are not absolutely and permanently defined but are interpreted according to the way they are used. The way words are used is, according to Wittgenstein, illuminated by the particular 'language game' within which they are employed. By language game, he meant the type of discourse in which people are engaged. Thus there might be a scientific language game; a theological language game; a psychological language game; and so on. These language games might share some word usage with or without the same meaning. The word 'belief' might have different connotations in psychology and theology.

As interpreters of language, it is necessary for us to recognise these cautionary considerations as we try to extract the fullest meaning from language that we receive from others. Unless we resort to Lefebvre's approach, of using a dead language within a highly ritualised context, we are bound to be expressing ourselves, communicating our views, signalling our emotions, through the medium of a living language. The words of this language are not fixed in their meaning and it is interesting to look at some of the methods that may be used to secure meaning, to anchor it to certain words...

There is no doubt that words migrate from one language game to another, from one type of discourse to another. In so doing, they possibly enrich the concepts of the new game by dragging across something of the old game. They may also bring across implications, or overtones of meaning, that do not fit so well into the new game.

60

Meaning and the education game

...Any honest attempt to communicate will be bedevilled by the additional unwanted overtones. It is perhaps the combination of words that have partially duplicating overtones, which permits the highly skilled communicator to convey meaning with more precision. It is also possible to want to communicate in a way that is not too precise. Some of the most poetic or stirring writing in a language requires the writer to surprise the reader with choices of words. The use of metaphor can be refreshing; ambiguity can heighten the significance of text as the reader or hearer plays around with the possible meaning. To use language in these ways is to play a different language game. These belong to the creative language game, whereas we are describing the straight communication language game.

This is not to say that metaphor has no place in straight communication. Andrew Wilkinson draws attention to an article by WJ Cheverst, who describes three groups of metaphors to be found in educational writing. Wilkinson writes:

> *In that which is* child-centred *we find words like 'growth', 'harmony', 'discovery', 'assimilation', 'readiness'. In that which is* knowledge-centred *we find words like 'store', 'foundation', 'stock', 'cells', 'bricks', 'structure'. In that which is* teacher-centred *there are words like 'guiding', 'shaping', 'moulding', 'directing', 'imparting'.*
>
> (Wilkinson, 1975)

It is possible to argue that these metaphors are words that have been taken from other language games, and that as knowledge 'seeps' from one context into another, so does meaning. It is a process that is both enriching and impoverishing, since it can be argued that by using a word out of its specific context, some of its original specificity is lost...

It is not possible to put artificial boundaries around words..., but it is not surprising that people attempt to do so. Sharing the specificity of meaning that some words have in some language games provides a form of identity for a group of people. Orthodoxy is very often a linguistic matter. Through the choice of metaphor, individuals communicate to others that their underpinning ideas are similar and, perhaps, conform to some group norm.

All of us involved in the process of education have words that we use, codes that identify us as educationalists. Sometimes these words take the form of initials, particularly infuriating to those not initiated, since without the key it is impossible to crack the code and one remains on the outside. PTR is one example. TVE is another. Try talking to someone with no connections with education about CPVE, NCC, LEATGS, or PSME. In psychology, the initials are just as difficult – ABA and S-R learning. Is this all about shorthand? Is it simply a matter of those with similar reference points being able to shortcut much of the language in order to concentrate on the bits that convey the real information? That may well be part of it, but there is a less charitable interpretation that this is a form of linguistic protectionism.

Just as we pointed out in relation to the use of legitimate and illegitimate means of influencing the views of others, it is not easy to decide whether the use of particular terms is intended to restrict access to meaning, to close ranks in the face of the outsider, or whether it is a genuine way of assuming common reference points. In practice, it depends on an analysis of the linguistic context, including a study of the interactions prior to the present one.

Negotiating meaning

What we have said about language so far points us towards a specific conclusion. We have indicated that, within the framework of a living language, the meaning of a word is not absolutely clear. It has to be inferred from the context, by reference to the language game that governs the discourse and to the interaction between the parties involved. Another way of putting this is to say that meaning is negotiable. What sense you make of what I say, can only be clarified if you ask me to explain what I mean and, indeed, if I ask you to tell me whether you have understood, or what you have understood. Meaning requires commentary, in the sense of explanation. Wittgenstein wrote:

> *If language is to be a means of communication there must be agreement not only in definitions but also (queer as this must sound) in judgements. This seems to abolish logic, but does not do so – it is one thing to describe methods of measurement, and another to obtain and state results of measurement. But what we call 'measuring' is partly determined by a certain constancy in results of measurement.*

> (Wittgenstein, 1984:88)

Agreement in the meaning of words, in the meaning of what we say to one another, leads us towards the view that knowledge is social, that our understanding of the world that we communicate to others is subject to a process of interpersonal interpretation. The value of the science language game or the logic language game is that words are used only after considerable care has been given to their definition. None the less, misinterpretation and misleading use can occur. The safeguard is still to be found in the negotiation of meaning.

Although we place much of the onus on the transmitter of information, the receiver certainly bears some of the responsibility for the quality of communication. In counselling, it is an established practice to reflect back to the client what the client has been saying:

'Let me just see if I've got it clear what you've been telling me'
or
'So what you're saying is...'

The counsellor, in stating her interpretation of the picture so far, is checking that this interpretation is in line with what the client intended. A similar responsibility belongs to all of us receiving a message, especially when the message is ambiguous, conveys emotions, or causes emotions. It is in these circumstances that we are likely to stay silent or to give the message an interpretation that might not have been what the speaker intended. Each of us can produce a running commentary in our heads of the conversation that we are having. The commentary is an interaction at a thought level between what we hear and our own system for making sense of the world, which includes that conversation. Too often, we interpret silently and misinterpret. We get the other person wrong. The only way of preventing that is to seek clarification and to check out whether our interpretation is correct. These are difficult interpersonal skills. They are the basis for good communication, for good interpersonal relationships, and for team work. They may be crucial skills for young people to acquire and this causes us to consider how they can develop such skills.

The relevance of this view to educational practice shows itself in a number of ways. At one level, it provides a very important reason for teaching interpersonal skills. If people learn to regard meaning as something which cannot be taken for granted but which must be negotiated, then the quality of their interactions will be enhanced. At another level, such a view provides a rationale for the teacher in pursuing a questioning attitude towards the way language is used in text-books, in academic reference books, in policy documents, in their own lesson notes, hand-outs, and letters to parents. Adopting a more wary approach to language, how one uses it oneself, and how it is used by others, is a vital part of education for young people and forms one part of the approach that Postman and Weingartner (1969) call 'crap-detecting'.

The safeguarding of our political and intellectual freedoms may require teachers to show the next generation of students how to analyse language carefully in order to establish what is being communicated. At the very least, people need to feel a sense of unease with arguments that are too slick, and with communications that are heavily loaded so as to appeal to one's emotions rather than to one's reason. Spotting propaganda is a useful skill, but it might be also that out-and-out propaganda is easier to spot than the choice of certain metaphors, the employment of certain terms, and the reference to particular authority figures, as means of influence.

References

Atkinson JM (1984) *Our masters' voices: the language and body language of politics* Methuen
Heritage J & Greatbach D (1986) 'Generating applause: a study of rhetoric and response at party political conferences' *American Journal of Sociology* 92(2): pp110–157
Magee B (1987) *The great philosophers: an introduction to Western philosophy* BBC Books
Miller J (1983) *States of mind* BBC Books
Postman N & Weingartner C (1969) *Teaching as a subversive activity* Penguin
Thouless R (1974) *Straight and crooked thinking* Pan
Wilkinson A (1975) *Language and education* Oxford University Press
Wittgenstein L (1984) *Philosophical investigations* Blackwell

9.   Barriers to Communication

David Minton

In order to make progress in engaging students in the learning process, we must ensure that we and they recognise the barriers to learning they bring with them. We, as teachers, should be able to recognise specific problems students create for themselves or behavioural characteristics. It is not easy for us to see our own.

Mind-set and emotion

Emotional or attitudinal barriers result from cultural conditioning or response to past experience. We all have a mind-set about things that relate to us, a self-image that inhibits our willingness to believe we can do certain things, attitudes and beliefs we defend against overwhelming evidence.

Perhaps you know someone who is a banker. What image does that word conjure up for him or her, and for you? 'There are certain things bankers do, wear, enjoy, don't do, don't wear, don't enjoy, aren't there? I couldn't possibly...' and this will inhibit certain kinds of behaviour. Some girls (or their parents) still reject the idea of engineering as a career: 'Do women actually enjoy engineering or science or maths? Isn't that what men do, not women?' Some men believe that nursing or primary school teaching is an inappropriate choice of career. Where do such attitudes come from?

They clearly relate to our perception of ourselves, a powerful self-image we have developed as a result of our experience. Many, such as that of the banker, we derive from models around us. It is not unusual to meet students who genuinely see themselves as 'thick', not 'clever like these other people'. It may be a result of painful experiences in education in the past, or a defensive posture to protect them from possible failure.

We have our needs for personal space and territory. Our value-system, our likes and dislikes, are often firmly embedded: they are inextricable from 'me – who I am' and exhibited both in words and in body language. We can all read such body signals easily.

Someone who has a mind-set that says 'I can't do maths' is not going to succeed in maths, however hard the teacher tries, unless that mould can somehow be broken. This learner has had past experience of maths learning, perhaps reinforced with some role-model that has established a conviction that it is not worth trying. The same happens in most areas of learning. Ball games defeat some people utterly; some are all thumbs in craftwork; some are word-blind; some cannot draw a straight line. You will have heard people say these things. They are self-fulfilling prophecies.

It is far from easy to tackle such attitudinal barriers. Equally, when someone discovers a way through such a barrier, the effect on their self-image and on their lives can be quite dramatic.

Information theory

In 1949, the Shannon–Weaver mathematical theory of communication was published. These workers made a distinction between 'information' and 'informational channels': between what the information is about and the way it is transmitted, person to person. Shannon and Weaver were concerned to improve radar and radio transmission: 'We want to maintain a high-fidelity transmission so that messages don't get garbled on the way. We also want a lot of redundancy and clarity: we don't want noise interfering with the transmission.'

'Noise' and 'redundancy' are technical terms. Noise in radio is the jumble of background sound that may prevent us hearing what we are trying to listen to. We have all had the frustration of noise when we try to hear a concert or a talk on the radio; it can be even worse when television pictures break up, develop strange images or disappear. It is often referred to as interference. Redundancy refers to an excess deliberately put into the signal to ensure that something of the message gets through. The theory is about effectiveness in sending and receiving signals.

We are dealing here in metaphors, so this account is not be taken too literally. Problems in classrooms that affect information transmission, whatever the kind of signal, increase with distance. The further people are away, the harder it is for them to read our signals, for us to read theirs. So much of what we wish to share is to be read in the way we say or demonstrate it. Subtleties and nuances are lost.

Distraction in the classroom is one kind of 'noise'. For example, I was running a discussion with a group of teachers. A colleague who was with me said at the end that he had had great difficulty in concentrating on what I was saying because a woman sitting opposite him had such 'noisy legs'. After another session a group of students told me they found the design of the sweatshirt I was wearing so fascinating they simply couldn't follow my arguments.

Conflicting messages, emotional stress, aggressive behaviour may also act as 'noise'. The problem relates to the learner's 'attention'. Learners need to concentrate on what is to be learned, but so much can get in the way. Anything that interferes with attention is noise.

But so is lack of clarity in the signals and messages we wish to convey. The means of transmission – the tone of voice perhaps, the words we speak or the visual materials used – all need to be clear and easy to understand. Monotony of delivery will become 'noisy'. Rooms with difficult acoustics, rooms that are too hot, lighting conditions that prevent proper vision, seats that are too hard (or soft) can all get in the way of the message. Try to experience it as students do.

Redundancy implies that a message is so strong that it overcomes any noise likely to be around. A tale may be so absorbing that listeners ignore everything else; people can 'lose themselves' in a computer program, a book or a film. Most people are actually quite good at doing this.

Chaotic presentation of information with little or no structure will produce a great deal of noise. Ask yourself: How hard is this for students to understand? What exactly do I want them to take away? What can I get rid of so that they can grasp essentials presented?

It is notoriously difficult to write instruction manuals. Here again, structure is all-important. There has to be a clear learning path and action plan. Often a simplified diagram helps. And a correctly sequenced structure is vital. In one jet aircraft, the instructions to the pilot to eject were set out on the pilot's canopy: the first instruction was 'Eject the canopy'. Think about it...

Selection

The brain selects from experience. However hard we seem to be concentrating, we will select some things and ignore others. Teachers who recognise this can try to ensure that the important things do not get selected out. Repetition and redundancy, as already mentioned, are important here: hence the need for revisiting and consolidation.

A reasonably effective way of doing this is to get students to explain what they understand or what they have to do – what the thing is about or how it works. In trying to explain it to someone else there is not only an alerting of the brain, but also processing of what has been learned into the student's personal knowledge structure.

Repetition of material, revisiting, presentation of information in several different forms (OHTs, discussions, handouts) may be useful redundancy. It is very hard for students to grasp something they are only exposed to once.

Verbosity

Sheer volume of information is noisy. An overloaded channel or receiver obviously cannot cope. Have a look at the OHP transparencies you use. How much of the information can possibly get through, and how much is noise? What about the learning materials you use? Are they clear? Could you simplify it, make it easier to grasp? Could you structure it more clearly? How much is essential?

You need to be constantly alert to the problems of distraction and the need for clarity. *Less* may actually mean *better*. It is so easy to believe that the more that is said, the clearer it will be. Frequently, the opposite is true. Teachers tend to be verbose, to put too many words and symbols into OHP acetates or into instructions. Structure and key-words matter more than the information they contain. The message is: simplify it.

Incomplete information

The opposite problem can arise, however. Sometimes students are not given all the information they need by the teacher or the instruction card or the work-sheet or other task guidance. It is easy to make unjustified assumptions about what the learner knows already or will bring to the activity, or to fail to think through what it is that they need to know.

Using jargon can also lead to incompleteness. The purpose of jargon is to share understanding, to be unambiguous. It fails if the student does not know the words, or the symbols...

Language barriers

...It is easy to misunderstand someone if the words they use, even when they seem to be the same as words we use, carry all sorts of implications, references to values and expectations that are different from our own. We are not 'coming from the same place'. How much more likely is it when they use words or symbols which are less familiar to us! Do you in fact share the same cultural value system as your students? Even when you speak apparently the same language, are they interpreting your words as you intend?

Words can be said more accurately to have uses rather than meanings. There is a strong cultural element in all language use, so that it is almost impossible to understand a speaker of any language, including one's own(!), if you have no insight into the values and assumptions conveyed by the words he or she uses. All language works by accumulated meanings or nuances according to the context; we need to know who is using the word and for what purpose.

I remember one tutor telling me of an occasion when she was talking with a group about children and how important security was to them. She discovered after half an hour or so of discussion that some of the class thought she was talking about Social Security.

In many subject areas, there is a large specialist vocabulary to be learned. The use of symbols is vitally important in others. The meaning of the visual symbol is quite independent of the word that may be used to 'read' it. Consider the arabic numbers which may be expressed in many different words even in English let alone in other languages, but convey the same visual meaning. Jargon (which includes symbols) is intended to facilitate sharing between those who work in a particular field, but initially at least, jargon, specialist vocabulary, use of symbols and so on are more likely to confuse than to enlighten and may become a substitute for clear thinking...

Language register is also most important. We choose a style of speaking which is appropriate for the context we are in. We use a range of styles, words, phrases, sentence structures, formal and informal expressions and tones of voice. These are our 'language registers'. Consider the difference between making a speech at a wedding and chatting in the lounge with friends. Would you address your boss in the same way you would your husband or wife, or one of your children? Or your dog? What about your 'tone of voice'? In some cultures, choosing the right level of politeness in speech is more important than what is said. In others, anything goes apparently (though probably not!).

The words we use, our whole language register, show how we value the other person relative to others and ourselves. 'Talking down' to adults is to show that you do not value them as equal to yourself. On the other hand, if your choice of vocabulary is wrong, your sentence structures are too complex or idiosyncratic, or the speed at which you talk is too fast, you will fail to communicate with them...

Questions

Many classes seem to operate like the showing of holiday slides. There is no communication, because there is little sharing. Students are excluded. It is essential that they approach the experience alert and with a questioning brain. Humans are exploratory animals, so curiosity must be an important trait. If the brain operates by pattern-making and rule-making it must be searching to find the patterns and the rules. Exploring is a trait we share with the animal kingdom. Progress requires challenge, tackling and solving problems. Much of it is inherited behaviour; how else would you explain what beavers do?

What distinguishes humans is the ability to distance themselves from reality and to construct concepts – mental models that we describe in words. Exploratory, discovering activity is organised into concepts constructed to explain or control our experience.

It is this level of curiosity that questioning relates to. Most children are full of the word 'why?' A baby is asking a question when she puts a rattle in her mouth to explore hardness. Questions really require language, words, concepts; but would a child develop concepts without this physical exploration?

Questions have to do with alerting the brain to some new experience, idea or word-pattern that is coming and which might challenge our present understanding. Knowledge, according to Jerome Bruner in *The Process of Education* (1977), is a process of constant restructuring of concepts. It is not the lumps of stuff to transmit somehow from here to there. Nor can you just hammer knowledge into your students' brains: they must be ready to restructure, to deal with what is new. Information can only become personal knowledge when it is processed in some way. The radio must be switched on, as it were.

Without preparation the brain cannot deal with new information. It will ignore it, as it ignores most of the sensory data around us most of the time. We just do not notice it. We perceive consciously only the things we alert our brain to – the rest passes unnoticed and apparently unrecorded. That we have in fact recorded it can be shown by hypnosis, but concept formation depends on conscious alerting. What do you remember of the last twenty-four hours? Why those things and not all the rest?

Hence the importance of questions. Rote-learning, however powerful, actually has no effect on what people think or do. The learning is not part of our own structure of concepts, the way words work for us. It belongs to someone else.

Levels of questions

We can alert the brain to explore present experience or revisit past experience. Questions work at various levels:

- Level 1: direct experience – focusing on what is happening now
- Level 2: describing experience, to ourselves and to others; this is a second level of abstraction
- Level 3: comparing and interpreting experiences (a third level of abstraction) – this involves mental models/patterns; we restructure our conceptual understanding when patterns do match
- Level 4: thinking creatively, generalising, transferring learning to new contexts, using it to solve problems.

Much brain activity is to do with processing information. We may use questioning to make the brain receptive to take the information we want it to have and to provide us with perceptions of the world, and of our internal mental ideas. We need to do this all the time to be able to deal competently with our world.

But we can set the brain actively thinking to form new concepts and abstractions from experience, patterning information into new insights. There is a social function of language that allows us to share and bond: we experience this when we try to tell others how we are perceiving this information and experience – what we now know. We can compare it with the new structures they have created, and which they in turn express in their words.

This working with other people helps us to refine our ideas, to create hypotheses about the world and people that allow us to attempt to predict what will happen or what people will do. We need to explain and predict in order to try to control what happens. This is how technology works – and most human and social activity too. It is also how words acquire their meanings.

Teacher's questions

How can teachers handle questions? What should teachers do?

These two sentences are alerting statements, pseudo-questions, rhetorical questions: all teachers use them. They are not looking for creative response, but merely aiming to alert the students' brains.

They prepare them for 'my' answers, without stimulating them to find their own. Having a student actually discover answers different from 'mine' can seem to be bad news for many teachers. They want students to remember the 'right' answer, in other words 'mine'. Great weight is given to this procedure through the examination and testing system. The level of restructuring by the student depends not so much on curiosity as on extrinsic motivating factors such as the teacher's pleasure or anger, or passing the exam, or just 'getting it right'.

It depends critically too on how easy it is for the student to link the information or concepts into what is known already. If the pace of arrival of new information (or new words or new definitions) is too fast, or if the volume of information is overwhelming, learners cannot deal with it. In any case, just being exposed to it once will not work. It has to be revisited and rethought. It has to 'arrive' – to be put into familiar language or symbols. Teachers need to pitch it at the right level and recognise the barriers to learning that all of us have.

Effectiveness depends on the students' readiness to learn and on the control exercised by the teacher, who must manage pace and volume and the form in which the information is acquired. It must match the students' readiness and receptivity.

It is easier for learners if the structure is clear, and if it leads them through identifying questions which build from one to another, even if they are presented in the form of statements of key-words only. This will ensure alerting of the brain to deal with the information and assist processing.

Closed and open questions

Closed questions assume the 'right' answer exists. They can often be answered yes or no. Many tests are of this kind: true/false, objective tests, computations and so on. Much of education seems to be about closed questions. Teachers often have a preference for them in many of their classroom interactions.

As an alerting exercise a closed question can be successful. But to be effective as a technique the teacher must name students who are to answer. General questions addressed to the whole group are ineffective in alerting all students, since most will leave it to the clever-clogs to answer. It is realised that this is teacher's game: I don't want to play at guessing teacher's right answer. Why don't you just tell us, sir?

The teacher is not looking for competing answers, nor even for students to reframe the information into their own words. This last is vitally important and questioning can be used effectively to promote level 2 activity. The questions may still be closed. But if students are to achieve levels 3 or 4, they need open questions that stimulate them to think.

Inductive methodology is the use of open questions...

Open questions receive unpredictable answers: 'messing about here for a bit to see what we can discover'. Indeed their purpose is not to elicit answers at all, but to generate increasingly searching questions. Open questions are about an attitude of mind, stimulating natural curiosity to explore and find out.

They also involve openly valuing each student's answer, however improbable it might be. It is very easy to demotivate students from even trying to find answers or generate ideas. Most can experience damage to their self-esteem if they find themselves competing with others in discovery learning. The most successful approach is usually to set students up in groups to explore problems and ideas. They feel less exposed and can give mutual support.

A great deal of wasted effort is also caused by asking questions which are of the wrong kind, looking for unhelpful answers. First find the right questions and validate them to make sure they alert the students to useful activity, and they will look in the right sort of places.

Structured questions that define a linking path are better than a series of unconnected general questions, at least until students have sufficient experience to structure their own paths. But the students may still arrive at the 'wrong' answers or go off in the wrong direction. A teacher using inductive methods has to decide when to intervene, certainly if discovery learning is intended. Unlearning is much harder than learning, so students need to get it right first time. There is frustration in letting them get into a mess with it, nor should they be trying to re-invent the wheel.

The appropriateness or otherwise of discovery needs appraising. Again, it is a matter of clearly formulating what has to be done and controlling the learning activity through structure. The main purpose may be to promote group bonding rather than what they in fact discover for themselves...

References

Bruner J (1977) *The process of education* John Wiley

Shanon C & Weaver W (1949) *The mathematical theory of communication* University of Illinois Press

10.   Ergonomics / Human Factors

David Minton

Ergonomics (called 'human factors' in the United States) can be defined as 'managing work'. It is a study of the interaction of human beings with things they use and environments where they work. It is concerned with the amount of effort it costs to do something, and what can be done to make it more human, less inefficient in the way it affects the people concerned. All objects, or whole environments, intended for human use should be designed to take account of the human users, of what is supposed to happen and what is to be done there.

How often do teachers have to battle with badly designed rooms or workshops? How many are expected to teach in environments 'designed' on assumptions about what is going to happen as learning activity which are no longer valid? How hard is it for them to get things they need, or to do adequate preparation? How hard is it for the students too? How can you maintain motivation if it is too hard?

Certainly, industrialisation has forced workers into desperately uncomfortable, exhausting environments: noisy, machine-dominated, production orientated and inhuman. Think of the early cotton-mills; imagine what it was like to drive and stoke great steam engines on the railway, where a man had to shovel six tons of coal between Leeds and London while the engine bounced around at high speed. Until quite recently, factories survived where riveters had to work inside huge boilers with the result that they became deaf.

It is all grossly inefficient. The cost of the human has to be measured in with the cost of machines and buildings. As teachers we can try to ensure that factors under our control support what we ask the students to do rather than get in the way...

Personal space

Personal space is felt as an area surrounding a person's body in which there are boundaries for interactions with other people. It is defined by zones of social contact. The types of possible interaction vary with distance, which is shaped by the context and environment.

A study by Hall simplified this into concentric circles. He identified four zones: intimate, personal, social and public distances from the centre. [See diagram overleaf.]

The behaviour of a person whose space is violated may change considerably if the 'wrong' person enters a zone or if 'wrong' interactions are attempted there.

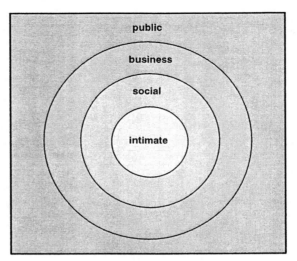

Personal space
(from Hall, 1959)

Closeness increases the effect of one person on another. There is increased sensory stimulation; smell and sound are added to sight. And the amounts of physical contact allowed between individuals varies in different cultures: for example, it seems greater among the French and Italians than the English, who like to keep each other at arm's length (a distance confirmed by research). Middle-class people seem to be more likely to hug and kiss each other than are the working class, and women more so than men – except on the football field, perhaps.

People who work together tend to use close social distance, while business is conducted more distantly. It has to do with seeing the whole person: with the enlargement and importance of the head as people approach, and with maintaining eye-contact. This distance is important also in screening out other people. Public distance is well outside a circle of social involvement, and at this distance other communication problems occur.

Establishing right relationships relates to identifying appropriate zones for social contacts. To be intimate in behaviour, one has to be close and to be comfortable there. Men and women behave differently in this zone. Invasion may seem threatening: there may be tension, discomfort or even flight. Drama training uses techniques to overcome such barriers to physical contact, and they are also broken down in sports like rugby. Working together in a physical way requires contact; indeed, team behaviour requires a redefining of everyone's personal space zones, perhaps creating group space instead.

A typical reaction to invasion of personal space is to face away, avoid eye contact, become stiff, pull in the shoulders – leave! Defensive behaviour is typified by lack of verbal response, or by abusiveness. Hall says, 'We treat space as we do sex. It is there, but we don't talk about it.'

Studies of crowding and empty space on trains identified a stress chemical in the urine of passengers who had travelled in crowded carriages. Invasion created responses that were complex, but intended to distance the intruder from the victim: leaning away, turning, or more simply withdrawing into oneself. In crowded trains people shrink their private space and control their discomfort by staring at the floor or into space: their body language projects non-relating to non-persons.

Territoriality

Concepts such as personal space and territoriality are borrowed from behavioural analyses of animals to explain how such factors may affect performance. You will have watched a dog mark out his territory. Most male animals seem to have some means of doing it, so why not humans? And is it only males?

Like personal space, territoriality is a concept that has social, unwritten rules of space behaviour. Infringing these rules will cause discomfort and often hostility. Territoriality differs from personal space in that territories are fixed locations, and do not move around with the people who define them. The boundaries are sensory, marked by stimuli such as scent in animals, and visible cues such as coats and bags with humans. You will see students mark out their territories in this way. Why do people feel more comfortable if they always use the same seat or table?

We all know the rules that govern territory. We can all distinguish that which is 'mine', such as a house or flat which can be controlled even when 'I' am not there, from that which is for everyone, like a park, and from that which becomes semi-private – claimed by someone on a temporary basis, such as a seat on a train.

Behaviour related to semi-private territory is of importance to teachers. It appears when students reserve seats and mark seat boundaries in a class with 'ownership' of equipment. Studies in trains showed there was little verbal exchange; passengers had territory markers like bags and coats on the adjacent seat. Students use bags and books. An invader is forced to ask for a marker to be removed – 'is this seat taken?' Removing it oneself breaks the social code.

Well-designed teaching spaces need to take into account not only the more obvious things (often ignored, though), such as acoustics, noise levels, temperature control and ventilation, but also the spaces that are occupied for particular purposes. Teaching spaces may be rendered ineffective if seating arrangements are such that students are unable to mark territories (they can't spread out), or if they feel impelled to withdraw into themselves to preserve their need for personal space. Density and crowding are threatening both to personal space and territoriality. Having too many students in a class also makes social grouping difficult.

Teachers need to control the spaces students occupy. They should try to define group territories where they want group activities. Having students sitting in rows merely defines the teacher's space.

...We need to be constantly watching: what are the messages we are giving and what are our students' reactions to them? If students define group territories, we should make sure they are used to good and effective purpose.

Activity has to be planned in relation to physical distance, eye-contact, territorial identification of working groups and their resources. It needs to be restructured frequently to prevent the fixing of small cliques, and to ensure that space is right for each particular learning activity. Variety is important...

It is up to you, as teacher, to take control, to establish the rules for group behaviour, to define territories if need be by moving people around, to set up different groupings for varied activity. And whatever you do, do not let groups settle into one fixed pattern.

Managing your group

Watch your class carefully as it becomes a social group, and in particular if people join the group late. What happens? Why?

What action should you take if they form not one cohesive group, but several cliques? How will you ensure they come together and agree purpose, goals, rules, patterns of sharing and working as a team together? How will you help them define their boundaries?

Community

Human beings are social animals. Communication is 'sharing' within a community: a group with defined boundaries, shared purposes and duties, and a common language.

Exploring and social behaviour

Learning is an activity on the part of learners in which teachers may play a minor role. We talk about a picture, or a building or a statue, communicating with a person. What can we mean? Clearly, pictures just hang there. The energy for anything to happen has to come from the viewer, whatever skill the artist had...

Joining groups

In looking for the bases of communication, we should bear in mind the idea of the group with boundaries. Competition between groups will define boundaries more sharply. Members of each group will invent all sorts of glue and banners to proclaim 'us' against 'them'. In extremes, it can turn into secret societies with hand-shakes and coded signalling, but frequently it is a matter of dress or uniform and other open signals. In most societies we recognise groups that adopt pseudo-military uniform indications of rank: the police, fire service, ambulance service, nurses and so on. When people put on a particular uniform they also adopt a behaviour pattern with it.

One hidden purpose is to ensure that 'the whole is greater than the sum of the parts'. Groups that gel – that is, that work well together – achieve much more than the same individuals would on their own. Where does this added value come from?

We can see analogies in the animal world. Some are mysterious. The ant-hill, created by termites, is a remarkable structure with a complex ventilation system including chimneys that heat up and extract stale air, so generating air currents through the tunnels. But where is the 'model in the head' that enables termites to build it? There is no possibility of the parts existing alone, so how do individual termites know in their tiny blind world what each has to do to construct the whole? Communication, we know, is by chemical pheromones excreted by the queen. In human groups too there is a mystery as to how purposes and direction arise, and how they are communicated to all involved.

Joining a sports team carries with it the competitive element. A team spirit is exhibited in dress and observation of specific rules and codes. It is derived partly from agreed purposes (goals!) and partly from perceived antagonists (other teams). Team members rely on the others, and display a commitment to the team that supersedes other social commitments. The same is true of a drama group or an orchestra. We exploit this competitive glue in setting up learning games.

Group behaviour imposes a need for individuals to discover a role in the group. This is no less true for you, as teacher, than for any other members, unless you choose to remain as an 'outsider'. To be the disruptive outsider cannot be right.

To be effective, you will have to establish that you are working with the students as part of a group while you are together – to be one of 'us'. The unhappiest experience you can have as a teacher is to find a group ganging up against you and to be fighting to establish common ground. Your own behaviour may even help to create that distance. Your first job as the teacher is to establish the class as a group with agreed goals, roles, rules of behaving and responsibilities.

We may think of an evening class as a club. Complicated things may be going on. There are rules which govern the operation of the club: what are they for? how are they arrived at? Anyone joining has to learn and observe them and has to take trouble to see what this means. People who have dealt with adult groups know that breaking into established groups is difficult and disruptive.

It is easier if the rules are stated explicitly, but important ones are usually exhibited only in the behaviour of the club members: what is considered acceptable and what is not. Peer group pressure and a desire to become, or remain, one of the group ensure that members learn rules quickly. New members arrive feeling 'foreign', but wanting to be accepted as one of 'us'. They look constantly for clues as to how to behave and are extremely sensitive to modelling and feedback: they will conform in dress and language use, even if it feels odd or wrong. They will absorb values and ways of thinking too.

Sharing

Sharing is clearly an important aspect of communication. Searching, wanting to share and to belong is another. Being part of a group, or a valued and effective member of a team, working with others to achieve a goal is all part of our sense of community. Being an outsider is a painful experience. Being isolated by language or cultural differences is also highly disturbing, particularly if it involves loss of self-respect because you can no longer do things for yourself, such as use the telephone or order a meal. This can happen in joining new groups or classes at home as well as when we travel abroad.

In many aspects of communication, the energy has to come principally from you. We are more acutely aware of this in activities we do alone than in those we share with others. In looking at pictures or walking through a city, we respond in individual ways to the stimuli about us. We may quickly get bored or we may experience a high level of excitement, depending on our receptivity to the stimuli. In other situations, even if we are totally passive, as when listening to a concert in a concert hall, or watching a play, or an opera maybe, on stage in a theatre, we are infected by shared emotional responses. Rock concerts make these shared responses much more uninhibited and dominant.

Television has become the major source of entertainment world-wide and has had a profound effect on the traditional cultures of many peoples. Though for us it tends to be a 'private' experience, except when sharing the excitement of a crowd watching a football match, say, it absorbs us like reading an interesting book. We share experience not just with those who make the programmes; we know many other people are sharing it, too. It is such a powerful educational tool mainly because we learn more readily if our attention is strongly focused, and we are not putting up barriers to the learning. We do not know that we are learning, we are 'having fun'.

References

Hall ET (1959) *Silent language* Fawcett, Premier Books

Communication Strategies in Teaching

Using the word 'strategies' to describe the interaction which teachers employ in the classroom suggests that we employ deliberate processes of planning and control. Research supports the view that the personal communication style of the teacher is the crucial factor in determining the balance between teacher authority and student freedom in any given lesson or learning encounter, though the nature of the programme of study itself – traditional academic or outcomes-based – will also have an important effect. There is an interesting – though perhaps predictable – tension between the desire of most learners to be given more responsibility and the wish of most teachers to limit learner autonomy.

Specific research projects involving detailed observation of classroom discourse in, for example, the teaching of English and in medical training indicate the nature of the constraints which are placed upon students by the directive and controlling language behaviour of teachers. The analysis of such lessons shows that teachers tend to plan within the boundaries of what they can realistically expect to control. Variables which determine the communication strategies used include the prior experience, understanding and expectations of the learners, the relationships between teachers and students within an institution, and sometimes even those between adults and young people in society at large.

Examples of interaction in English classes indicate that discourse follows very clear strategies, designed by the teachers to assert their power and to control how the students interpret the subject. The teachers present prescribed knowledge and opinions, explore how the students are dealing with that, and at the end of the lesson cause the discourse to return for teacher refinement and reinterpretation. Most of the evidence confirms that the locus of power remains firmly with the teacher.

Existing inequalities in power (e.g. teacher-student, interviewer-interviewee) are reinforced by the communication style selected by the leading participant, and teachers habitually use forms of language which would be regarded as condescending – if not insolent – in other encounters. Many of us have been reproved at home for exactly this offence.

An awareness of appropriate communication styles should not be confined to the use of language, though. Our non-verbal cues are often more significant than our actual words. Tone of voice, posture, gesture, dress all give out messages which may compete with – and sometimes even subvert – the content of our speech. No study of communication can be complete without some understanding of the non-verbal aspects of our social behaviour.

11. The Communication Styles of Teachers in Post-Compulsory Education

Joe Harkin & Pauline Davis

I was recently commenting sourly to a colleague in psychology on the proclivity of educators to fasten on some small pieces of research – for example on 'discovery' or 'creativity' – and to puff it up into an educational panacea. He remarked wryly that teaching was such an uphill job that teachers have to have some sort of a booster every five or ten years to keep their spirits up. Bible texts are no longer any good, so snippets of research have to do instead!

(R S Peters, 1973)

This paper sets out some preliminary findings of a current research project that is investigating the communication styles in British post-compulsory education.

The project arises out of a number of concerns. First of all, the advent of the outcome-based programmes, such as NVQ, GNVQ and the Enterprise in Higher Education initiative, has been accompanied by an expectation that they will give rise to greater learner responsibility and freedom (Haffenden & Brown, 1989; Jessup, 1991). If this is the case, this should be evident in changed patterns of communication between teachers and learners. Secondly, the development of communication as a core skill for learners in post-compulsory education is partly dependent on the dominant patterns of communication used by teachers – what are these patterns, and do they facilitate the development of learners' communication skills? Thirdly, the training of teachers in the further and higher education sectors is often based upon the reflective practice model. Reflection by teachers about how they communicate with learners may be facilitated by providing a conceptual framework.

The research model

The project is based on two strategies: the use of investigating instruments developed by researchers at the University of Utrecht and their collaborators in other countries; and the use of classroom observation of communication, influenced by the work of a range of people who have carried out research into classroom talk, such as Flanders, Barnes, Coulthard and Swann.

The questionnaire on Teacher Interaction (QTI) developed at Utrecht has now been used many thousands of times, for over a decade, in many countries, and has been tested for reliability and validity in several separate studies (Wubbels, 1993). It is based on a model of Interpersonal Teacher Behaviour that takes a systems approach in which teacher behaviour both influences and is influenced by learner behaviour. It is assumed that every form of behaviour communicates a message about 'content' and about the relationship between teacher and learner, so behaviour is measured against two dimensions: a *Proximity* dimension (Co-operation-Opposition) and an *Influence* dimension (Dominance-Submission). These terms, translated from the Dutch by the Dutch researchers, may carry different connotations in English to those intended, nevertheless, two key dimensions of interaction between teachers and learners are highlighted: the balance between teachers and learners of *control* of classroom interaction and the dominant *ethos* of the interaction. The two are not, of course, mutually exclusive but together form a profile of teacher interaction.

Teacher behaviour is characterised into eight profile types [appendix, taken from Brekelmans, 1994], some of which (types 1-3) are more conducive to effective learning than others. These types (directive; authoritative; and tolerant/authoritative) create a purposeful and coherent structure for learning in which, especially in types 2 and 3, there is a positive ethos of co-operation between teachers and learners.

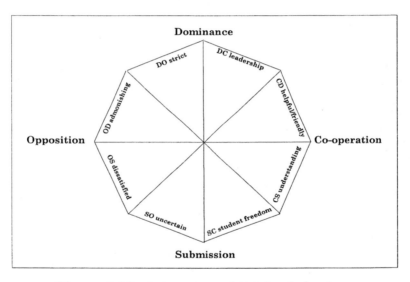

The model for interpersonal teacher behaviour
(from Brekelmans, 1994)

The Utrecht data indicates that, especially for older learners (i.e. teenagers onwards) a trade-off must be made between teacher dominance (strictness and leadership – which correlate with high levels of student achievement) and helping/friendly and understanding behaviours which meet student expectations of an appropriate ethos for learning. Thus type 2 and 3 profiles represent an 'ideal' balance of interaction for teachers in post-compulsory education.

The English sample

Three colleges of further education were selected to participate in the study – a large, urban college; a smaller, semi-rural college; and a tertiary college in a market town. Staff were invited to volunteer to take part by identifying two groups of learners with whom they work, with different characteristics, preferably one group on an outcome-based programme, and the other on a more traditional programme. When no outcome-based programme was taught, teachers were asked to substitute an 'in-between' programme, such as a BTEC course, which would become an outcome-based programme in time. The teachers and the students then each completed three 48-item questionnaires. So far, over fifty teachers and five hundred students have completed the questionnaires.

The fact that participants were volunteers will affect the results of the study. The comparative Dutch data indicates that, as may be expected, volunteers are closer to the 'ideal' types than teachers in general.

Participating teachers were also asked if they were willing to be observed teaching. For this purpose video was used, together with a computer-based recording system using a 15-item inventory of communication behaviours.

A first analysis of the data is being carried out using SPSS, the Statistical Package for Social Sciences. Descriptive statistics, non-parametric tests and correlational analysis have been used to gain a picture of both the teachers' and the learners' perceptions of actual, ideal and worst teacher communication styles. It is intended to carry out a multivariate analysis of the data, using the first analysis to highlight areas of interest. This will overcome problems, such as missing data values and the non-normality of the data, that were encountered when basing the analysis on one random variable.

The preliminary findings

First of all, the good news. There is a lot of evidence that teachers in further education are doing a good job. There is a lot of agreement between students' and teachers' perceptions of ideal and actual behaviour. Most teachers are actually type 2 and hold an ideal model that is type 3, i.e. they believe that ideally they should get closer to the students, display more helping/friendly and understanding behaviours and generally create a warmer supportive ethos for learning, but there is not a great disparity between teachers' ideal conceptions of their role and their actual practice. This is matched by the students' perceptions; they too perceive most of their teachers as type 2, and also hold type 3 as an ideal model.

Within this generally happy picture there are findings that give rise to a need for further enquiry and debate. In general, teachers overestimate all their behaviours, that is they believe that their behaviours in every category are more marked than they are in fact perceived to be by learners. This may be in line with research (Fraser, 1987; Wubbels, 1993) that shows that teacher behaviour – although it does make a significant difference to individual learners – is a small factor in educational achievement when compared with socio-economic factors, student ability and previous achievement. Teachers may simply overestimate their influence on learners. Another possible explanation is that teachers, like people in general, may be rather solipsistically bound up in their own self-perceptions.

Comparing teacher and learner ideal models of teacher behaviour, learners in general want teachers to be more like the teachers' *perceptions* of how they believe they actually behave. In other words, most learners are happy with their teachers, but would like them to be more leadership orientated, more helpful and friendly, and more understanding – all of which are in line with the actual and ideal models held by the teachers themselves.

However, there is one significant area in which learner and teacher perceptions are diametrically opposed: learners, on all types of programmes, would like to be given more responsibility and freedom, whereas teachers would prefer to give them less. Furthermore, the studies at the University of Utrecht (Wubbels, 1993) found that it is particularly difficult for older, more experienced, teachers to share responsibility with learners and a tendency to wish to be 'in control' (associated with leadership and strict behaviours) tends to increase. In the three colleges we studied, most teachers currently employed are in the older age categories, which may reflect the national demography of teachers in post-compulsory education.

In their responses, students showed themselves to want teachers to structure learning and to keep them on task – they are happy that teachers should be 'strict' when necessary, and in control of the learning process. However, linked with this teacher-led approach, learners wished to be able to decide more of the things they do and to have more positive influence over the learning process.

It may be thought that the instrumental and pragmatic nature of further education, orientated as it is towards adulthood and work, gives rise to a pure transmission model of the curriculum, in which the role of the teacher is simply to transmit skills, knowledge and understanding to learners, in an ethos in which affectivity is minimal. The results of the research so far show this to be far from the truth. Both learners and teachers wish the ethos of learning to be purposeful but at the same time to possess a 'human face', marked by the ability of teachers to share a joke, respond to individual need, explain points more than once if necessary, and treat learners as responsible partners in the learning process. This desire is more marked among learners than it is among teachers. The latter are drawn also towards more controlling behaviours that in fact lessen rather than increase student responsibility and freedom – much teacher communication is about overt or covert *control* of the interaction.

Overt control includes determining what will be done during the lesson, and at what pace, by making open statements; and intervening to bring learners back on target when their attention wanders. Covert control is established and maintained by a wide variety of means: the structure of the lesson; where the teacher stands or sits; who the teacher talks with; control of writing on the board; the asking of rhetorical questions intended ostensibly to elicit understanding; the use of dictation; the setting of tasks for their own sake; the use of marker words, such as *Right: OK* to re-assert control and continue with the teacher's lesson plan.

Thus there appears to be a tension for many teachers between what seem to be conflicting desires – to have a warm, supportive ethos that promotes student engagement in the process of learning; and to exert a lot of control over the process of learning that uses strict behaviours to limit learner autonomy. This tension is exemplified by the marked absence of the use of students' personal names by teachers, despite the fact that nearly all teachers state that their preferred behaviour is to address students by their first names. It was in fact rare to find a teacher who used first names more than occasionally. Similarly, learners rarely addressed their teachers by name.

The thrust of new initiatives in further and higher education is that learners should take more responsibility for their own learning. This is a feature of NVQs, GNVQs and the Enterprise in Higher Education scheme and arises from a mixture of ideological, pedagogical and pragmatic reasons – ideologically it may be desirable to empower learners; pedagogically, more active participation by learners in the learning process may result in longer term and deeper learning; pragmatically, the recruitment of more learners with less per capita resource means that it may not be possible to teach and learn in traditional ways.

If it is thought desirable to give learners more responsibility for their own learning, then teachers need to learn how to share their power. *Control* behaviours (which are not altogether inappropriate) need to be tempered with other behaviours, especially a combination of leader-ship with more *helpful/friendly* and *understanding* behaviours. A fundamental shift is required in some cases which will not be easy, especially for older teachers, from teacher-dominated to teacher-sharing lessons. This shift would be accompanied by significant changes in language (towards more adult-adult exchanges) and affectivity (towards more use of personal names and acknowledgement of feelings).

The research findings so far indicate that there is a difference between the amount of responsibility and freedom given to students on outcome-based, 'in-between' and traditional programmes; and a difference also in the amount of leadership displayed by teachers. Teachers on outcome-based programmes give students more responsibility and freedom, whilst at the same time exhibiting more leadership behaviours. The students on outcome-based programmes indicated that they have more autonomy than students on other types of course, whilst they find that their teachers explain things more clearly, act more confidently and talk more enthusiastically about the subject. In other words, teachers on outcome-based programmes seem to 'lead' more effectively and to give learners more autonomy.

In response to questions about leadership and learner autonomy, there was a perceptible progression from traditional programmes, such as A levels, which were the least highly regarded, through BTEC programmes – which were in general perceived by learners to be much more satisfactory – to outcome-based programmes, where learner satisfaction was highest... It appears that there is little difference in learner decision making between A level/GCSE and BTEC type programmes, whereas GNVQ programmes increase learner autonomy.

The explanation of these differences needs to be approached with care and further research needs to be carried out. Do outcome-based programmes make both the teacher-led management of learning (leadership) and student autonomy (responsibility and freedom) inevitable? Learners share with teachers an understanding of the expected outcomes, and help to monitor their own performance. In the early stages of setting up outcome-based programmes are only the more 'effective' teachers getting involved? Are the teachers on outcome-based programmes in general younger and, because of this, display more enthusiasm for the subject and for sharing responsibilities with learners? The results so far indicate that there are differences between the *same* teachers on different types of programme – indicating that the structure of the programme itself may be an important factor.

Although the picture that emerges of teacher behaviour is generally a happy one, a need for more adequate staff development opportunities for teachers is highlighted by the finding that, although most teachers are perceived to be effective, a quarter of the sample fell into types that are not satisfactory – types 5, 6, 7 and 8 – and that display characteristics associated by teachers and learners with the *worst* kinds of teacher behaviour. Typically, these teachers are expending precious energy that should be directed at teaching (and therefore learning) into control behaviours; sometimes a struggle for control that is wearing for both teacher and students. Bearing in mind that the research was based on the work of volunteer teachers, and that the Dutch data shows that the general population of teachers are on average less effective, this finding gives cause for concern. It is likely that more than one in four teachers in further education are perceived by their students as being seriously deficient. At a time of great curriculum change, when so many teachers are under high levels of stress (NFER, 1994), there is an urgent need for adequate systems of staff support, guidance and development.

Participation in a course of teacher training, such as the Certificate in Education for Teachers in Further Education, may give rise to improvements in the performance of teachers, at least for the duration of the programme. Teachers on an in-service Certificate programme were perceived by their students to show greater leadership, and were more helpful, friendly and understanding, and were less uncertain, dissatisfied and strict than other teachers. However, it is unclear how long these benefits last – there appears to be little difference between trained and untrained teachers in the general sample. More work will need to be carried out on this topic but there may be a case for emphasising the need for updating and refresher courses, especially for teachers who have been in service for many years, and more especially at times of intense curriculum change. This supports the views of Eraut (1994) who found that the front-loading of professional training does not match the actual patterns of development of professional knowledge. The research continues to explore these and other issues, in the hope that greater clarity and insight into teacher behaviours will provide teachers with a better basis for professional reflection and judgement and, through this process, that learners may be given better opportunities to learn.

References

Brekelmans M (1994) 'Interpersonal behaviour of teachers in the first decade of their professional careers' Paper to the Twentieth Annual Conference of the British Educational Research Association, Oxford

Eraut M (1994) *Developing professional knowledge and competence* Falmer

Fraser BJ (1987) 'Synthesis of educational productivity research' *International Journal of Educational Research* 28

Haffenden I & Brown A (1989) 'Towards the implementation of competence based curricula in colleges of FE' in T Burke *Competency based education and training* Falmer: pp132–170

Jessup G (1991) *Outcomes: NVQs and the emerging model of education and training* Falmer

NFER (1994) 'Survey into stress in post-compulsory education' carried out on behalf of NATFHE *NATFHE Journal* Autumn: pp4–5

Peters RS (1973) *The philosophy of education* Oxford University Press

Wubbels T (1993) *Do you know what you look like? Interpersonal relationships in education* Falmer

Appendix

Interpersonal profiles of the eight types of the typology of interpersonal styles

1) Directive

The learning environment in a class with a teacher with a directive profile is well structured and task-oriented. The directive teacher is organised efficiently and normally completes all lessons on time. S/he dominates class discussion, but generally holds students' interest. The teacher usually isn't really close to the students, though s/he is occasionally friendly and understanding. S/he has high standards and is seen as demanding. While things seem businesslike, the teacher continually has to work at it. S/he gets angry at times and has to remind the class that they are there to work. S/he likes to call on students who misbehave and are inattentive. This normally straightens them up quickly.

2) Authoritative

The authoritative atmosphere is well structured, pleasant and task-oriented. Rules and procedures are clear and students don't need to be reminded. They are attentive, and generally produce better work than their peers in the directive teacher's classes. The authoritative teacher is enthusiastic and open to students' needs, s/he takes a personal interest in them, and this comes through in the lessons. While his/her favourite method is the lecture, the authoritative teacher frequently uses other techniques. The lessons are well planned and logically structured.

3) Tolerant and authoritative

Tolerant and authoritative teachers maintain a structure which supports student responsibility and freedom. They use a variety of methods, to which students respond well. They frequently organise their lessons around small group work. While the class environment resembles Type 2, the tolerant/authoritative teacher develops closer relationships with students. They enjoy the class and are highly involved in most lessons. Both students and teacher can occasionally be seen laughing, and there is very little need to enforce the rules. The teacher ignores minor disruptions, choosing instead to concentrate on the lesson. Students work to reach their own and the teacher's instructional goals with little or no complaints.

4) Tolerant

There seem to be separate Dutch and American views of the tolerant teacher. To the Dutch, the atmosphere is pleasant and supportive and students enjoy attending class. They have more freedom in type 4 classes than in those above, and have some real power to influence curriculum and instruction. Students appreciate the teacher's personal involvement and his/her ability to match the subject matter with their learning styles. They often work at their own pace and the class atmosphere sometimes may be a little confused as a result.

In the US, however, the tolerant teacher is seen to be disorganised. His/her lessons are not prepared well and they don't challenge students. The teacher often begins the lesson with an explanation and then sends the students off to individually complete an assignment. While the teacher is interested in students' personal lives, his/her academic expectations for them aren't evident.

5) Uncertain/tolerant

Uncertain/tolerant teachers are highly co-operative but don't show much leadership in class. Their lessons are poorly structured, are not introduced completely and don't have much follow-through. They generally tolerate disorder, and students are not task-oriented. The uncertain/tolerant teacher is quite concerned about the class, and is willing to explain things repeatedly to students who haven't been listening. The atmosphere is so unstructured, however, that only the students in front are attentive while the others play games, do homework and the like. They are not provocative, however, and the teacher manages to ignore them while loudly and quickly covering the subject. The uncertain/tolerant teacher's rules of behaviour are arbitrary, and students don't know what to expect when infractions occur. The teacher's few efforts to stop the misbehaviour are delivered without emphasis and have little effect on the class. Sometimes the teacher reacts quickly, and at other times completely ignores inattentiveness. Class performance expectations are minimal and mostly immediate rather than long range. The overall effect is of an unproductive equilibrium in which teacher and students seem to go their own way.

6) Uncertain/aggressive

These classes are characterised by an aggressive kind of disorder. Teacher and students regard each other as opponents and spend almost all their time in symmetrically escalating conflicts. Students seize nearly every opportunity to be disruptive, and continually provoke the teacher by jumping up, laughing and shouting out. This generally brings a panicked over-reaction from the teacher which is met by even greater student misbehaviour. An observer in this class might see the teacher and students fighting over a book which the student has been reading. The teacher grabs the book in an effort to force the student to pay attention. The student resists because s/he thinks the teacher has no right to his/her property. Since neither one backs down, the situation often escalates out of control. In the middle of the confusion the uncertain/aggressive teacher may suddenly try to discipline a few students, but often manages to miss the real culprit. Because of the teacher's unpredictable and unbalanced behaviour the students feel that he/she is to blame. Rules of behaviour aren't communicated or explained properly. The teacher spends most of his/her time trying to manage the class, yet seems unwilling to experiment with different instructional techniques. S/he prefers to think *'first, they'll have to behave'*. Learning is the least important aspect of the class, unfortunately.

7) Repressive

Students in the repressive teacher's class are uninvolved and extremely docile. They follow the rules and are afraid of the teacher's angry outbursts. S/he seems to overreact to small transgressions, frequently making sarcastic remarks or giving failing grades. The repressive teacher is the epitome of complementary rigidity. The repressive teacher's lessons are structured but not well-organised. While directions and background information are provided, few questions are allowed or encouraged. Occasionally, students will work on individual assignments, for which they receive precious little help from the teacher. The atmosphere is guarded and unpleasant and the students are apprehensive and fearful. Since the repressive teacher's expectations are competition-oriented and inflated, students worry a lot about their exams. The teacher seems to repress student initiative, preferring to lecture while the students sit still. They perceive the teacher as unhappy and impatient and their silence seems like the calm before the storm.

8) Drudging

The atmosphere in a drudging teacher's class varies between type 5 and 6 disorder. One thing is constant however: the teacher continually struggles to manage the class. S/he usually succeeds (unlike types 5 and 6), but not before expending a great deal of energy. Students pay attention as long as the teacher actively tries to motivate them. When they do not get involved, the atmosphere is oriented toward the subject matter and the teacher doesn't generate much warmth. S/he generally follows a routine in which s/he does most of the talking and avoids experimenting with new methods. The drudging teacher always seems is be going downhill and the class is neither enthusiastic nor supportive nor competitive. Unfortunately, because of the continual concern with class management the teacher sometimes looks as though s/he is on the verge of burn out.

12.   The Discourse of Post-16 English Teaching

Frank Hardman & John Williamson

ABSTRACT *The discourse styles of 10 teachers of post-16 English from the north-east of England were intensively analysed using a descriptive system adapted from the study of discourse analysis. It was found that teacher-led recitation, which research suggests dominates classroom practice in mainstream schooling, was also a prominent feature in post-16 English teaching. The linguistic and cognitive constraints imposed on students by the pervasive use of the recitation script are considered together with the need for more qualitative analysis of classroom talk in order to promote wider communicative and cognitively demanding options.*

Introduction

Until the mid-1980s the teaching of post-16 English in England had mainly consisted of the study of literary texts selected from a traditional canon of English literature, and the explicit study of the nature and functions of language had not been a feature in the curriculum. However, the introduction of a separate advanced certificate ('A' level) in English language was seen as a major innovation in developing post-16 literacy because of its emphasis on knowledge about language and the uses of English: by such means students would increase their competences in its uses.

Commentators on the teaching of post-16 English (e.g. Whiteley, 1990; Harrison & Mountford, 1992; McCulloch *et al*, 1993; Canwell & Ogborn, 1994; Blue, 1995) assume that 'discussion' is a regular classroom activity in both subjects. Such an assumption about post-16 English teaching goes back to the already nostalgic image of 'intellectual discipleship' of the *Crowther Report* (Crowther, 1959), where 'subject-minded' students are introduced to scholarship through the mediating influence of a specialist teacher's knowledge. In such rhetoric on post-16 English teaching it is assumed that on the route to 'mastery' of an academic craft, whether in the study of language or literature, there must be increasing opportunities to display a growing acquisition of the skills in specialised speech and writing and to demonstrate them without close direction. It is also assumed that studying English at this level carries with it the right to question as students acquire some of the working practices of the subject and participate in their discourses. Therefore, the ideal post-16 English lesson is often conceived as being a seminar in which the teacher is no more than a leading participant in a process of discovery.

According to Dillon (1974), however, 'real' discussion, in which there is the exploration of a topic or issue and interchange of ideas with no predetermined outcome, is rarely practised in schools because of the domination of teacher-led recitation. In its prototypical form recitation consists of three moves: an *initiation*, usually in the form of a teacher question, a *response*, in which a student attempts to answer the question, and a *follow-up* move, in which the teacher provides some form of feedback (very often in the form of an evaluation) to the student's response. The frequency of this 'I-R-F format' (the variant 'I-R-E' is preferred by some writers because of the high level of evaluation and for the purposes of the present article it will be denoted I-R-F/E) and the overwhelming tendency of teachers to make the first and third move is what makes classroom discourse so distinctive.

Within the I-R-F/E structure the teacher usually holds the floor by controlling the turn-taking, presenting 'closed' questions to students and deciding who will answer and how, thereby providing little opportunity for student-initiated discussion. This distinctive feature of classroom discourse results from the teacher's claim to all the knowledge of the business in hand, which the students normally concede, so that teachers routinely ask questions to which they already know the answer and set the limits within which an acceptable answer must fall. It is the teacher who defines the area of knowledge and controls the discourse, with the students' task being to discover what s/he has in mind rather than generating ideas of their own. Therefore, the I-R-F/E format does not socialise the students into confirming, extending or challenging the knowledge being presented and, because it does not allow for genuine discussion, access to the joint construction of knowledge is withheld and the students are dependent on the teacher for classroom meanings instead of developing their own ideas.

Most of the evidence supporting the conclusion of the ubiquity of the three part exchange structure in classroom discussion comes from mainstream schooling (see Edwards & Westage, 1994, for a review of the evidence). It is, therefore, difficult to generalise from this finding in the post-16 context, where it is assumed teaching conditions are often different because of smaller classes made up of more motivated students. However, there is surprisingly little empirical evidence about how students are taught and how they learn in English at the post-16 level. The widest survey of classroom practice that does exist, although with little theoretical or empirical justification, comes from Her Majesty's Inspectors (Department of Education and Science, 1986) and is limited to the teaching of English literature (English language was not offered as a separate subject until the mid 1980s). In their account of how the subject is taught HMI found that students often had a passive role because of teaching preoccupied with the requirements of the final examination. They therefore found 'a considerable amount of teacher monologue in evidence' and questioning techniques which 'were sometimes narrow or obscure, with a preconceived notion of the 'correct' answer' (DES, 1986: 8). This, they report, often resulted in teacher domination of the classroom discourse, with little interactional space for students and a narrow range of written work with little opportunity for wider reading. Therefore, it would seem that teacher-controlled 'recitation' of prescribed knowledge, which research suggests is the predominant pedagogy in mainstream schooling, also persists into post-16 English literature teaching.

The Study

Given the lack of empirical evidence into the nature of classroom discourse in the post-16 English curriculum, an intensive study of 10 teachers who taught English language and English literature was carried out. The teachers, who ranged in teaching experience from 2 to 32 years, were drawn from six comprehensive schools and a large tertiary college serving urban, small town and rural areas in the north-east of England. Each of the teachers was video-recorded as they taught a complete English language and English literature lesson (20 lessons in total making up over 22 hours of video tape). The lessons were then analysed using a framework adapted from Sinclair & Coulthard's (1992) system of discourse analysis. The study also investigated, using semi-structured interviews, how the teachers perceived their teaching of the two subjects, where all reported that they regularly used classroom discussion.

The descriptive apparatus for spoken discourse developed by Sinclair & Coulthard proposes that lessons can be analysed as having five *ranks*: lesson, transaction, exchange, move, act. A lesson consists of one or more *transactions,* which consist of one or more *exchanges,* which consists of one or more *moves,* which consists of one or more *acts.* The study analysed the discourse at the rank of the exchange, as it is here that Sinclair & Coulthard are confident that the system is more reliable as it draws on linguistic considerations in describing what is going on.

Sinclair & Coulthard identify 11 subcategories of teaching exchanges with specific functions and unique structures. Of the 11 subcategories six are *free* exchanges and five are *bound.* The function of bound exchanges is fixed because they are not initiating moves, whereas the free exchanges can be initiated by the teacher or, as in two cases, by the students. The four main functions of exchanges are informing, directing, eliciting and checking. The *teacher inform* exchange is used for passing on facts, opinions, ideas and new information to the students and usually there is no verbal response to the initiation. The *teacher direct* is designed to get the students to do but not say something, whereas the *teacher elicit* is designed to get a verbal contribution from the students. The elicit exchange which occurs inside the classroom has a different function from most occurring outside it because the teacher usually knows the answer to the question which is being asked. This accounts for the *feedback* move being an essential element in an eliciting exchange inside the classroom because the students, having given their answer, want to know if it was correct.

Although *student elicit* is listed as one of the free exchanges, Sinclair & Coulthard acknowledge that inside the classroom students rarely ask questions and if they do they are usually of a procedural nature. The crucial difference between teacher and student elicits is that students usually provide no feedback as evaluation of a teacher's reply would normally be seen as deviant. Occasionally students offer information which they think is relevant or interesting and they usually receive an evaluation and comment on its worth. The final free exchange is the *check,* which teachers will use to check on how well students are getting on, whether they are following the lesson and whether they can hear; feedback to such questions is not essential as they are real questions to which the teacher does not know the answer.

Of the five types of bound exchanges, four are bound to teacher elicits and one to teacher direct. With a *re-initiation* exchange, if the teacher gets no response to an elicitation he or she can rephrase a question or use a prompt, nomination or clue to get a reply to the original question. Alternatively, if the teacher gets a wrong answer the choice can be to stay with the same student and try by the 'Socratic' method to work round to the right answer or stay with the same question and move on to another student. Here feedback does occur in the exchange. If the teacher withholds evaluation until two or three answers have been provided such an exchange is categorised as a *listing*. In situations when someone does not hear or where the teacher has heard but wants the reply repeated for some reason the exchange is classified as a *repeat*. Finally, in the bound exchange there is a *reinforce* which very occasionally follows a teacher direct when a teacher has told the class to do something and one student is slow or reluctant or hasn't fully understood.

Findings

The framework of analysis adopted by the present study provided a clear and systematic basis for analysing the classroom discourse in all 20 lessons because for the majority of the time linguistic interaction centred on the teacher was the main activity. Having transcribed and coded the lessons according to the system of analysis developed by Sinclair & Coulthard (1992) the teaching exchanges could be quantified and turned into percentage scores for comparison. The figure below shows the overall distributions of teaching exchanges used in the language and literature lessons.

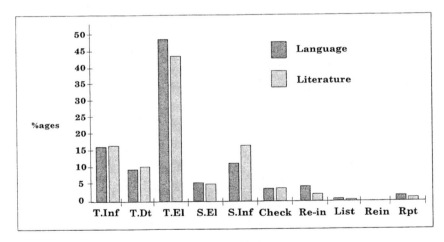

Exchange Types

Overall percentage scores of teaching exchanges for all 10 teachers. T.Inf - teacher inform; T.Dt - teacher direct; T.El - teacher elicit; S.El - student elicit; S.Inf - student inform; Re-in - re-initiate; List - listing; Rein - reinforce; Rpt - repeat.

The analysis of the discourse in all 20 lessons revealed that all 10 teachers worked within an I-R-F/E format across both subjects. There was an overwhelming predominance of teacher-directed question-and-answer and teacher presentation, as reflected in the high level of *teacher eliciting* and *teacher informing* exchanges, which account for 65 and 61% of the total teaching exchanges in language and literature respectively. The findings also show that there is little variation in the teaching styles of the 10 teachers as they taught across the two 'A' level English subjects. This supports an extensive statistical survey of students' perception of the instructional practices employed by teachers in language and literature lessons, which also found little variation in the range of teaching and learning activities employed and where it was found that 'class discussion' occurred almost every lesson (Tymms & Vincent, 1995).

The discourse analysis of the 20 lessons therefore challenges the general assumption discussed earlier about the nature of 'classroom discussion' in post-16 English lessons, where 'good practice' is often conceived as being a seminar in which the teacher is no more than a leading participant and mediating influence in a process of discovery. Such a notion assumes that students have the right to challenge and question as they acquire some of the working practices of the subject and participate in the subject discourse. However, *student elicits* account for just 5 and 4% of the teaching exchanges in the language and literature lesson respectively, suggesting that exploration of a topic through questioning by the students so as to allow an interchange of ideas was rarely practised.

The analysis of the teaching exchanges suggests that all 20 lessons were conducted through teacher recitation where interrogation of the students' knowledge and understanding was the most common form of teacher/student interaction. This is illustrated in the following example taken from the early stages of a language lesson where the teacher is looking for invented words in an extract from *A Clockwork Orange*. The *moves* (Initiation, Response, Feedback) make up the three-part teaching exchange, which in turn are made up of *acts:* acc, accept; ack, acknowledge; ch, check; cl, clue; com, comment; con, conclusion; d, direct; e, evaluation; el, elicitation; i, inform; l, loop; m, marker; ms, metastatement; n, nomination; p, a prompt; rea, react; rep, reply; s, starter; z, aside. Different stages in lessons are signalled by *boundary* exchanges consisting of *moves: framing* (Fr) and *focusing* (Fs), both of which can occur together.

Exchanges			Moves	Acts
Boundary	T	right	Fr	m
		let's see if we can err agree here upon words and even better if we can identify the parts of speech here i.e. nouns verbs adjectives adverbs and let's see if some words are now more frequently substituted than others	Fs	ms
Teaching	T	Paula you start us off	I	s
		which is the first word you say is invented		el
3	S	auto it's not really invented it's putting it a different way		rep
4	T	yeah	F	e
5	T	auto is	I	s
		are we going to count that invented word or substitute		el

6	S	substitute	R	rep
7	T	yeah short form of automobile actually at one time almost a slang word for a car an auto ok so question mark over that	F	e com

It shows the predictable teacher-student sequence and brief, fast exchanges that characterise teacher-led recitation, with the students being called on to display their knowledge through responding to teacher-initiated dialogue and questions. Student responses to these elicitations are then either positively or negatively evaluated by the teacher for accuracy, form and appropriateness against some predetermined answer.

While the teachers were often seen asking complex questions which showed a high level of thinking on their part, for the student as responder the question was often a request for information which did not require advanced cognition. All that was usually required from the student was a brief answer which reflected back what was in the teacher's mind. This is illustrated in the following extract from a literature lesson. The teacher's stated objective was to get the students to actively explore the characters in the mechanicals scene from *A Midsummer Night's Dream* by getting them to stage the scene. However, because of his questioning technique, what should have been a problem for the students soon becomes a problem for the teacher, with the students having to work out what is in his mind.

Exchanges			Moves	Acts
Boundary	T	ok	Fr	m
Teaching		let's move on	I	d
3		we've discussed Bottom then let's come over here and ask Quince	I	s
				s
		who's Quince here		el
		what kind of person do you think you are		el
4	S	erm very sort of calm and trying to keep	R	rep
5	T	urm hum	F	e
6		but you're already suggested you can't win with Bottom	I	el
7	S	well you've just got to (inaudible)	R	rep
8	T	you see I think you get Bottom to do what you want him to do in here	I	s
		which is what		el
		what do you want Bottom to do Quince		el
9	S	erm play the role you've given him	R	rep
10	T	which was that of	I	el
11	S	Pyramus	R	rep
12	T	Pyramus the lover yes	F	e
13	T	how do you get Bottom in the end to accept that he's going to do that	I	s

	T	look at the bit where you get Bottom to do that		cl
		can I share with you where does it come where		el
		you actually get Bottom to do that part		
14	S	line seventy three	R	rep
15	T	line	I	l
16	S	seventy three	R	rep
17	T	it's whether it's the first part you distribute	I	s
		isn't it Pyramus and it's the last one that you		
		eventually get settled now doesn't that that		s
		does tell you something about Bottom doesn't		
		it that he interrupts that he interferes that		
		wants to be everything he's full of life		
		I've also seen a production incidentally where		s
		he's a thorough pain in the neck he's irritation		
		to everyone as they want to get on with it and		
		he won't let them		
		but how it is handled at the bottom of page		el
		fifty one by Quince		
18	S	he tries to make him sound really good so that	R	rep
		erm he's one of the best you know he's the		
		best person in the play		
19	T	yeah	F	e
20	T	so what is he using as a technique	I	s
		what is he using		el
21	S	he just praises Pyramus so it looks as if it's the	R	rep
		best part		
22	T	right yeah	F	e
23	T	and therefore	I	s
		you still haven't got the word I want		el
24	S	he's flattering him	R	rep
25	T	he's	I	l
26	S	flattering him	R	rep
27	T	yeah he is flattering him isn't he	F	e
		and saying that there's nobody here but you		com
		who can do this		
28		and look what Bottom's reply is top of that	I	s
		page		i
		you know you might pause for a moment and		
		think to keep him on a knife's edge well you		
		know I undertake it you know big of you you		
		know I'll do it but you've got Quince yes you've		
		got the cast that you wanted at that point but		
		you had to flatter him in order to do it		

In this extract the teacher is seen building up to an elicitation through starter acts (e.g. Turn 17) designed to help the students arrive at the 'correct' answer and this kind of questioning sequence is routinely produced throughout all 20 lessons. If the question is not answered to the teacher's satisfaction, the teacher can 'reformulate' the question and go on doing so until an acceptable answer has been achieved (Turns 20-27). The extract also illustrates the length of turn (e.g. Turns 17 and 28) which teachers usually take compared to students' brief responses and which often develop into mini-lectures, giving them an unequal share of the talking space to the detriment of all other participants.

Four of the teachers appeared, however, to allow more space for students to contribute their ideas through *student informing* exchanges, which account for 11 and 17% of the overall teaching exchanges in the language and literature lessons respectively. This can be seen in the following extract taken from a literature lesson in which a student is making a presentation on the character of Autolycus from *A Winter's Tale*.

Exchanges				Moves	Acts
Teaching	S	right		I	m
		and then he spots the clown on page eighty three line thirty five and then he goes about robbing			i
2	S	erm after his robbing on line one hundred and fourteen he states he's going to the sheep festival this is really important to the plot direction of the play because if he doesn't go to the sheep shearing festival then		I	i
3	S	which line which page		I	el
4	S	page ninety five no I've lost it where's it gone err page eighty seven		R	rep
5	S	if he didn't go to the sheep shearing festival then nothing that would be the end of the play wouldn't it because then you there wouldn't the Shepherd and the Clown go to Sicilia and the father wouldn't be presented before Leontes and then the reconciliation between his daughter wouldn't happen		I	i
6	T	urm that's very true isn't it as far as the direction of the plot is concerned Autolycus plays a very important part there		F	e / com
7	T	carry on Tony excellent		I	d
8	S	yeah and we move on to scene four act four err lines five hundred and ninety six to six hundred here he talks about how honesty is a fool and trust is his sworn brother and it's quite important to like to his character to show like how devious he is		I	i
9	S	and then on page one hundred and twenty five there's he's seen by and forty seven and that's quite important to the play as well		I	i

10	T	say why	I	el
11	S	because then he wouldn't be able to con the Clown and the Shepherd again by saying I'm going to take you to see Leontes	R	rep
12	T	yes it's become a disguise of that of a lord yes	F	e
13	S	erm on line six hundred and seventy on the next page he understands and erm realises what's going on between Camillo Florizel and Perdita and he then begins to on the next page to con the Shepherd and the Clown and this takes a while	I	i
14	S	he talks about the father on line seven hundred and seventeen which is on	I	i
15	T	what's this parcel again you keep referring to	I	el
16	S	a parcel of what Antigonus left for next to the baby of Perdita	R	rep
17	T	which is important why	I	el
18	S	because it tells them who did it	R	rep
19	T	yes it does that's right	F	e

Although the student is expected to 'lead' the seminar discussion through his presentation, the analysis suggests it does not result in the other students asking questions and making extended, thoughtful comments of their own so as to develop the argument. In this extract the only question asked by a student is a procedural question (Turn 3), enquiring about the page reference. In contrast to this, the teacher asks questions (Turns 10, 15 and 17) to confirm, extend and challenge the information being provided, the answers to which are typically evaluated and commented on (Turns 6, 12 and 19).

In this way the teacher exerts his control over the discourse: although he appears to be using a more decentralised form of teacher-student interaction to promote a greater student engagement and participation in the classroom talk, a closer look at the discourse suggests there is little change to the I-R-F/E format. It is the teacher who asserts his 'right' as the 'expert' to control the frame of reference and there is little scope for student initiatives leading to a lessening of interactional or semantic control by the teacher. The teacher's continued use of questions for initiating, extending and controlling the discourse and his use of the *feedback* move to evaluate the student's contribution means that the students' contributions are not being extended so as to draw out their significance, make wider connections and encourage a greater equality of student participation.

Conclusion and implications

The findings of the current study reveal that the post-16 English curriculum is dominated by transmissional forms of teaching in which recall or comprehension of authoritative information are the main goals. It also shows little variation in the teaching styles of the 10 teachers as they teach across the two English subjects at this level. Therefore, 'normal' classroom discourse is recitation, where typically the teacher asks a series of preplanned questions, initiates all the topics and rarely interacts with the substance of the students' answers except to evaluate them. As a result, 'real' discussion as defined by Dillon (1994), in which there is the exploration of a topic and interchange of ideas to enable higher order thinking, seems to be rarely practised. Clearly this has implications for the range of roles students can play in the classroom discourse and for their linguistic and cognitive development.

Research into the constructivist function of dialogue and learning suggests that classroom discourse is not effective unless students play an active part in their learning (see for example Barnes & Todd, 1995). This social constructivist view of learning suggests that our most important learning does not take place through the addition of discrete facts to an existing store but by relating new information, new experiences, new ways of understanding to existing understanding of the matter in hand. One of the most important ways of working on this understanding is through talk, particularly where students are given the opportunity to assume greater control over their own learning by initiating ideas and responses which consequently promotes articulate thinking. If the student is allowed to contribute to the shaping of the verbal agenda in this way, then this is found to be more effective in developing the students' own cognitive framework. According to this widely accepted view of learning, such an approach should also allow for alternative frames of reference which are open to negotiation and where the criteria of relevance are not imposed. It therefore questions the value of the linguistic and cognitive demands made on students within the traditional I-R-F/E format, as demonstrated in the present study, where the students are mainly expected to be passive and to recall, when asked, what they have learned and to report other people's thinking. The social constructivist view of learning therefore suggests students' linguistic and cognitive development may benefit from wider communicative options.

Similarly, Cazden (1995: p159) suggests that the constructivist model is increasingly being seen in terms of the requirements being made of students entering higher education and the labour market because of the social and economic developments in most advanced societies demanding that schools develop 'deeper understanding of knowledge, greater flexibility of skills, and more interpersonal competences for all students than many of the élite achieved in the past'. Therefore, in much of the literature surrounding the teaching of post-16 English discussion is seen as playing a vital role in developing 'transferable skills' needed in preparation for either higher education or employment. In other words, it is seen as encouraging initiative and autonomy.

However, the ubiquity of the three-part exchange structure in all 20 A-level English lessons minimised the amount of responsibility which the students were able to take for their own learning in both subject areas, as they were usually dependent on the teacher's sense of relevance. In other words, it was the teacher as the authority figure who defined the 'truth', with the students making suggestions as to what they thought the truth, as the teacher sees it, might have been. The three-part structure, with its series of initiations, responses and evaluations, was often used by the teachers to facilitate the students' assertion of the points that they wanted them to make so that the evaluation move was frequently used to acknowledge some suggestions but reject or correct others in order to guide the students towards an appropriate version of the truth as they see it. The teacher was, therefore, often seen retaining control over the direction and pace of the lesson and the lines of knowledge which were to be pursued.

Such findings also depart considerably from notions of 'subject-minded' students discussed earlier, who at this level are expected to be independent and self-reliant in their learning and able to articulate and think for themselves, because of the expectation that most would go on to higher education. The teacher-led recitation, which was a common feature of all 20 lessons, therefore limited the extent to which students could develop their oral skills and critical thinking and take responsibility for their own learning. Such skills are seen by many commentators (e.g. Harrison & Mountford, 1992; McCulloch *et al*, 1993) as being essential, particularly for those students continuing in full-time academic education who are largely destined for occupations demanding 'leadership' qualities and higher order thinking skills. It is for these reasons that the didactic teaching methods revealed in the current study have often been regarded as inappropriate for inducting able students into the ways of the subject discipline, because it is thought that they fail to develop higher order thinking skills and conceptual understanding.

The findings of the current study, pointing to a lack of fit between the teachers' perceptions of how they taught the two subjects and classroom practice, suggest the need for monitoring and self-evaluation to become a regular part of initial and in-service training. They also suggest the need for the exploration and researching of alternative teaching and learning strategies which will help to raise the quality of teachers' interactions with their students and which will promote wider communicative (and hence more cognitively demanding) options to those in which students are often mere listeners or respondents within an I-R-F/E mode. Dillon (1994) and Westgate & Hughes (1997) suggest that talk analysis feedback may be a useful tool whereby sympathetic discussion by groups of teachers of data (recordings and transcriptions) derived from their own classrooms could be an effective starting point for professional development. Barnes & Todd (1995: 105) also argue that research, as in the present study, will need to go hand-in-hand with professional development for teachers since 'beginning to set up opportunities for students to learn through collaborative talk is much more than a change in their perception of their own roles and those of students in the process of teaching and learning'. As the present study suggests, this is a challenging agenda requiring evidence from classroom contexts analysed by qualitative approaches and markers of 'quality' which do justice to the contextual complexities of the classroom.

References

Barnes D & Todd F (1995) *Communication and learning revisited: making meaning through talk* Heinemann

Blue G (1995) 'Language after sixteen' in C Brumfit ed *Language education in the National Curriculum* Blackwell

Canwell S & Ogborn J (1994) 'Balancing the books: modes of assessment in A level English literature' in S Brindley ed *Teaching English* Open University Press

Cazden CB (1995) 'Visible and invisible pedagogics in literacy education' in P Atkinson, B Davies & S Delamont eds *Discourse and reproduction* Hampton Press

Crowther W (1959) *Crowther Report: fifteen to eighteen* HMSO

Department of Education and Science (1986) *A survey of the teaching of 'A' level English literature in 20 mixed sixth forms in comprehensive schools* HMSO

Dillon JT (1994) *Using discussion in classrooms* Open University Press

Edwards AD & Westgate DPG (1994) *Investigating classroom talk* 2nd edn Falmer Press

Harrison BT & Mountford D (1992) 'Consultative patterns of guided teaming in English post-16 studies' *Educational Review* 42: pp195–204

McCulloch R, Mathieson M & Powis V (1993) *English 16–19: entitlement at A-level* David Fulton

Sinclair J & Coulthard M (1992) 'Towards an analysis of discourse' in M Coulthard ed *Advances in spoken discourse analysis* Routledge

Tymms PB & Vincent L (1995) *Comparing examination boards and syllabuses at A-Level: students' grades, attitudes and perceptions of classroom processes* Northern Ireland Council for the Curriculum, Examinations and Assessment

Westgate D & Hughes M (1997) 'Identifying "quality" in classroom talk: an enduring research task' *Language and Education* 11: pp125–139

Whiteley M (1990) 'Whither A-level literature?' in: NATE Post-16 Committee ed *A-level English pressures for change* National Association for the Teaching of English

13. Discourse and Power

Norman Fairclough

The purpose of this chapter is to explore various dimensions of the relations of power and language...

This section on power in discourse is concerned with discourse as a place where relations of power are actually exercised and enacted; I discuss power in 'face-to-face' spoken discourse [and] power in 'cross-cultural' discourse where participants belong to different ethnic groupings...

Power in discourse

Let us begin the discussion of power in discourse with an example of the exercise of power in a type of 'face-to-face' discourse where participants are unequal – what we might call an *unequal encounter*. The following is an extract from a visit to a premature baby unit by a doctor (D) and a group of medical students (S), as part of the students' training programme. A spaced dot indicates a short pause, a dash a longer pause, bold square brackets overlap, and parentheses talk which was not distinguishable enough to transcribe.

(1) D: and let's gather round . the first of the infants – now what I want you to do is to make a basic . neo-natal examination just as Dr Mathews has to do as soon as a baby arrives in the ward . all right so you are actually going to get your hands on the infant . and look at the key points and demonstrate them to the group as you're doing it will you do that for me please . off you go

(2) S: well first of all I'm going to ⌈( )

(3) D: ⌊first . before you do that is do you wash your hands isn't it I . cos you've just been examining another baby (long silence) are you still in a are you in a position to start examining yet ( )

(4) S: just going to remove this .

(5) D: very good . it's putting it back that's the problem isn't it eh –

(6) S: come back Mum —

(7) D: that's right. OK now just get a little more room by shifting baby . er up the . thing a bit more that's very good . well now . off you go and describe what's going on

(8) S: well here's a young baby boy . who we've decided is thirty . thirty seven weeks old now . was born . two weeks ago . um is fairly active . his er eyes are open . he's got hair on . his head .

⌈his eyes are ⌈open

(9) D: ⌊yes   ⌊yes you've told me that

(10) S: um he's crying or ⌈making

(11) D: ⌊yeah we we we we've heard that now what other examination are you going to make I mean –

103

(12) S: erm we'll see if he'll respond to

(13) D: now look . did we not look at a baby with a
       head problem yesterday .

(14) S: right

(15) D: and might you not make one examination of the head almost at square one .
       before you begin .

(16) S: feel for the ( )

(17) D: now what ⌈ . the next most important thing .

(18) S: ⌊ . er   gross mo –
       gross motor   ⌈ function

(19) D: ⌊well now you come down to the mouth don't we.

(20) S: yes

(21) D: now what about the mouth

(The Boys from Horseferry Road, Granada Television 1980)

One immediately striking feature, marked by the square brackets, is the number of times the doctor interrupts the student – in (3), (9), (11), (13), and (19). (There are no square brackets in (13), because there is no actual overlap.) My impression is that the doctor does not interrupt simply because he wants to do all the talking, as people sometimes do. I think he interrupts in order to *control* the contributions of the student – to stop him beginning the examination before washing his hands, to stop him repeating information or giving obvious and irrelevant information, to ensure the student gives the key information expected.

In what other ways does the doctor exercise control over the student's contributions?

Firstly, in the opening turn, where the nature of what is going to go on in the interaction is announced to the students – including the nature of their own contributions. Secondly, in the way in which the student is explicitly told when to start talking and examining, at the end of turn (1) *(off you go)* and again in (7). Thirdly, in the equally explicit instructions to the student as to how he should sequence his actions, in (3). Fourthly, in the way in which the student's contributions are evaluated in (5) *(very good)* and (7) *(that's right);* positive and encouraging as they are, these are still techniques of control which would be regarded as presumptuous or arrogant if they were addressed to an equal or someone more powerful.

The fifth and final point is that the student is 'put on the spot' in the series of questions of turns (13), (15), (17) and (19). The questions constitute a strategically ordered sequence which leads the student through the routine he has failed to master. Also, the student's obligation to answer is underscored in each case by a pause (marked by a spaced dot), brief silences in which all eyes are on him, and which it is definitely his responsibility to end!

Notice too the grammatical forms in which these questions are put: (13) and (15) are *negative questions - did we not?, might we not?* Using negative questions is sometimes (depending on intonation and other factors) like saying 'I assume that X is the case, but you seem to be suggesting it isn't; surely it is?' In this case, the student ought to know that X is the case, so asking him questions of this elaborate sort is a way of making him look silly. The power relationship is more baldly expressed in (17), where the reduced question forms (reduced, that is, from *now what do we do? what is the next most important thing?*) sound to me abrupt and curt. Finally, in (19) the doctor uses a *declarative* sentence rather than an *interrogative* sentence, with a *question tag: don't we?* The effect is rather like that of the negative questions.

On the basis of examples of this sort, we can say that power in discourse is to do with powerful participants *controlling and constraining the contributions of non-powerful participants.* It is useful to distinguish broadly between three types of such constraints – constraints on:

- *contents*, on what is said or done
- *relations*, the social relations people enter into in discourse
- *subjects*, or the 'subject positions' people can occupy.

'Relations' and 'subjects' are very closely connected, and all three overlap and co-occur in practice, but it is helpful to be able to distinguish them. Our example illustrates all three types of constraint. In terms of contents, the student is required to conduct an examination according to a learned routine, operating (relations) in a professional relationship to his audience and a subordinate relationship to the doctor, and occupying (subjects) the subject positions of (aspirant) doctor as well as student. These constraints imply particular linguistic forms.

But some of these constraints on the student do not appear to involve any direct control being exercised by the doctor. Notice for instance that all the *directive speech acts* (orders and questions) in the example come from the doctor: it appears that the doctor has the right to give orders and ask questions, whereas the students have only the obligation to comply and answer, in accordance with the subordinate relation of student to doctor. Yet the doctor is not directly controlling the student in this respect. Rather, the constraints derive from the conventions of the discourse type which is being drawn upon. However, in an indirect sense, the doctor *is* in control for it is the prerogative of powerful participants to determine which discourse type(s) may be legitimately drawn upon. Thus in addition to directly constraining contributions, powerful participants can indirectly constrain them by selecting the discourse type. Notice that the latter type of constraint is also a form of self-constraint: once a discourse type has been settled upon, its conventions apply to all participants, including the powerful ones. However, that is something of a simplification, because more powerful participants may be able to treat conventions in a more cavalier way, as well as to allow or disallow varying degrees of latitude to less powerful participants.

Power in cross-cultural encounters

In the example we have been looking at, I think it is safe to assume that the students are able to operate within the constraints on legitimate discourse type imposed by the doctor. But what about unequal encounters where the non-powerful people have cultural and linguistic backgrounds different from those of the powerful people? This is common for instance in 'gatekeeping encounters' – encounters such as a job interview in which a 'gatekeeper' who generally belongs to the societally dominant cultural grouping controls an encounter which determines whether someone gets a job, or gets access to some other valued objective. In contemporary Britain, for example, it is mainly white middle-class people who act as gatekeepers in gatekeeping encounters with members of the various ethnic (and cultural) minorities of Asian, West Indian, African, etc., origin.

Discourse types and orders of discourse vary across cultures. But in such gatekeeping encounters, white middle-class gatekeepers are likely to constrain the discourse types which can be drawn upon to those of the dominant cultural grouping. Sensitivity to cultural differences is growing in some cases, but slowly. Interviewers tend to assume, for instance, that interviewees are familiar with dominant ways of conducting interviews. And interviewees' contributions are correspondingly interpreted on the assumption that they are capable of working out what is required, and capable of providing it, in terms of these dominant conventions. So if an interviewee gives what is felt to be a poor or weak or irrelevant answer to a question, this is likely to be put down to her lack of the requisite knowledge or experience, her uncooperativeness, and so forth; the possibility of miscommunication because of differences in discoursal conventions rarely suggests itself. People may thus be denied jobs and other valuable social 'goods' through misconceptions based upon cultural insensitivity and dominance.

The possibilities for miscommunication are ample. For instance, the following snippet is from a simulated job interview for a post in a library with a member of an American cultural minority (C2):

Interviewer: What about the library interests you most?

C2:   What about the library in terms of the books? or the whole building?

Interviewer: Any point that you'd like to...

C2:   Oh, the children's books, because I have a child, and the children ... you know there's so many you know books for them to read you know, and little things that would interest them would interest me too.

(Akinasso FN & Ajirotutu CS 1982:124)

Notice that C2's English in terms of grammar and vocabulary is native-like, which in itself is likely to lead the interviewer to dismiss any thoughts of culturally based miscommunication even if those thoughts occurred. But that *is* a possibility. C2 has failed to interpret the interviewer's question in 'the obvious way' – as an invitation to C2 to show what she could do in her professional work in the library if appointed to the post. But 'the obvious way' is the way within a specific culture of 'the interview', and there is no inherent reason why people should not show how their work interests relate to their family and other interests in response to a question of this sort.

It may be justifiable to interpret as 'miscommunication' the outcome of individual interviews where people are denied jobs or other 'goods' partly on the basis of cultural differences. But such outcomes are more regular and more systematic than that would imply, and they would appear to be based upon not only cultural differences in discourse but also upon more overt differences in skin colour and lifestyle. Power in discourse between members of different cultural groupings is in this perspective an element in the domination of, particularly, black and Asian minorities by the white majority, and of institutionalised racism.

...I [have probably given] the impression that there is a great deal more homogeneity within cultural groupings then there really is. In fact, many white working-class British people from the dominant cultural grouping are as unfamiliar with the conventions of interviewing as members of black or Asian communities. But it is increasingly the case, as a result of the spread of interviewing practices across social institutions and the more intensive use of them within many institutions, that everybody is expected to be able to deal with interviews – from the interviewee end, of course! Those who cannot, either because of their cultural experience or because they belong to generations for which access to interviewing was constrained, are likely to be socially disabled.

The educational system has the major immediate responsibility for differentials in access. In the words of Michel Foucault, 'any system of education is a political way of maintaining or modifying the appropriation of discourses, along with the knowledges and powers which they carry'. And what is striking is the extent to which, despite the claims of education to differentiate only on the grounds of merit, differentiation follows social class lines: the higher one goes in the educational system, the greater the predominance of people from capitalist, 'middle-class', and professional backgrounds. The educational system reproduces without dramatic change the existing social division of labour, and the existing system of class relations. However, it will not do to blame the education system for constraints on access, or to attribute to it alone power over access. This power is diversified through the various social institutions, not just education, and its origins are ... in the system of class relations at societal level.

References

Akinasso FN & Ajirotutu CS (1982) 'Performance and ethnic style in job interviews' in J Gumperz ed *Language and social identity* Cambridge University Press
Granada Television (1980) *The boys from Horseferry Road*

14. Non-Verbal Communication

Nicky Hayes

Have you ever noticed how much you can say without words? We do it all the time. We communicate by gestures, tones of voice and facial expressions. And what about when you're choosing your clothes carefully for a special night out? What image are you trying to project? How is it different to the way you dress when you're going for a job interview? Most, if not all, human beings are expert in non-verbal communication. We are social animals, and like other social animals we spend most of our time in contact with other members of our species. This means that communication is extremely important, and we use more than one channel for it.

Non-verbal communication is usually specific to the context of the interaction. A shared glance with a friend can replace any amount of talking, but a glance exchanged with a stranger might not convey any message at all. So although researchers have been able to discuss the general meanings of non-verbal signals, the minutiae of non-verbal communication are far more complex, because they always depend on the shared social understandings and relationships which are relevant to that situation.

Non-verbal cues

Non-verbal communication can serve a number of social purposes. Argyle (1975) identified four of these, which are listed in Table 1. These different social purposes are achieved by using a range of cues, and it is worth looking at some of the main cues that we use in more detail.

Assisting speech
Such as emphasising important words by stressing them heavily, and saying them more slowly than other words

Replacing speech
For example, shrugging the shoulders to say 'I don't know'

Signalling attitudes
Such as adopting a bored facial expression when forced to listen to someone whose opinion you are not interested in

Signalling emotions
Such as hugging a close friend that you haven't seen for some time to express your pleasure at seeing them

---

Table 1 Functions of non-verbal communication
(from Argyle, 1975)

Facial expression

One of the more obvious forms of non-verbal cue which we use is facial expression. We greet someone we like with a smile, frown if we are puzzled, or scowl if we are angry. Human beings have immensely mobile faces, and can produce a large range of different expressions. Sometimes, these expressions are *idiosyncratic* – habitual expressions adopted by just one individual, or possibly by people in the same family. Everyone has their own distinctive way of smiling, for instance. Some expressions seem to be cultural in origin, used by people in that society but not elsewhere. But other facial expressions seem to be universal, found in all human cultures, which suggests that they may be innate.

In 1872, Darwin argued that the expression of basic emotions, such as hunger or fear, are innate, on the grounds that the same patterns occurred in other mammals as well as humans, implying that they had a common evolutionary origin. For example, the fear response in both humans and other mammals includes high-pitched whimpers and the pilomotor response, in which the hair stands on end. (In human beings, being relatively hairless, this shows itself as 'goose-pimples'.) This response occurs in dogs, cats, chimpanzees and monkeys, as well as in humans. Another of the distinctive features of fear is the 'fear-grin', in which the skin is pulled back from the teeth and the mouth is stretched wide, and this again is found in almost all mammals.

Other facial expressions may be inherited by human beings, but not necessarily by other animals. In an examination of several different films of social encounters made of people from different cultures, Eibl-Eiblesfeldt (1972) showed that a number of different facial expressions appeared in all these cultures. One of them was the 'eyebrow flash' of recognition: if we are greeting someone that we recognise, we raise our eyebrows quickly and lower them again. Osgood (1966) found that there seem to be seven main groups of facial expressions signalling emotions, which also seem to be universal for all human cultures. The seven groups are: surprise, fear, happiness, sadness, anger, interest and disgust or contempt.

Facial expression is also a powerful signal of attitudes, and in some respects this too may show links with other species. Van Lawick-Goodall (1974) observed that young chimpanzees show a 'play-face' which is very similar to the 'play-face' of children. It signals that what they are doing is a game, although human culture uses such signals in ways which seem to be rather more sophisticated than are found in chimpanzee cultures. Friedman *et al.* (1980) showed how the facial expressions of television presenters change to indicate approval or contempt, depending on the topic that they are discussing. This was particularly apparent during the 1976 American presidential elections, when presenters used different facial expressions when talking about Carter from those used when talking about Ford.

Eye-contact

Eye-contact is a powerful signal, which can signal both affection and hostility. Prolonged eye-contact with someone you love signals affection, but the same with a stranger is likely to be taken as a challenge. Ellsworth & Langer (1976) showed that prolonged gaze is very likely to invoke flight – people will withdraw from such a threatening situation. The fact that prolonged eye-contact is not easily ignored also tells us something about the power of non-verbal communication.

Eye-contact is also an important signal in regulating social interaction. Kendon (1967) observed pairs of students who were asked to 'get acquainted' with one another, and showed that we use quite a sophisticated set of social rules about eye-contact to regulate our conversations. For example, a speaker will tend to avoid eye-contact while she or he is speaking, but will look up at the end of an utterance, as if to 'hand over' to the other person. The listener, on the other hand, will look at the speaker much more. Argyle *et al.* (1968) showed that when normally sighted people were deprived of this cue because one of the pair was wearing dark glasses, conversations were much more hesitant and included more pauses and interruptions.

Breaking the conventional pattern may also be a signal in its own right. Dovidio & Ellyson (1982) showed how maintaining prolonged eye-contact while speaking, and looking away while listening, is a strategy people use to maintain social control over the interaction, and is a signal of power and status in social interaction...

Posture and gesture

Gestures are specific actions, usually made with the hands and arms during communication. They tend to be used to amplify and illustrate speech, and may have very precise, culturally specific meanings. For example, most Western cultures have a specific gesture to indicate that someone is 'crazy'. In some cultures, this is expressed by tapping the side of the forehead, but in others it is signalled by twirling the forefinger in the air by the side of the head. There are cultural differences, too, in the amount of gesture which is used: people from some cultures utilise a more expressive conversational style than those in others.

Posture involves the whole orientation of the body. Where gestures are often used to signal specific messages, posture is a powerful signal of general attitude – so powerful, indeed, that we will often take a message conveyed by posture as a much more reliable indicator of someone's attitude than what they say. We recognise, instantly, a casual posture, an aggressive stance or a relaxed, friendly position. One of the more interesting uses of posture in conversation occurs with the phenomenon known as *postural echo*. If we are talking to a friend or listening closely to someone else, we often unconsciously adopt the same posture that they are showing. It is thought that this provides an unconscious message that we are interested and on the same wavelength as they are.

McGinley *et al.* (1975) showed that the posture which someone adopts can make a difference both to whether we are likely to like them and to whether they are perceived as powerful. An open stance, like leaning back in a chair with legs extended and knees and feet apart, tends to be interpreted as more likeable as well as being a signal of confidence; more closed postures, such as having the legs or arms crossed, are seen as indicating that the person is being less open with us and more self-protective, therefore we are less likely to like them. Knapp *et al.* (1974) showed that minor self-grooming gestures, like running the fingers through the hair or touching the face, are often interpreted by observers as a sign of deception.

111

Proxemics

Hall (1968) described how we all learn very specific *proxemic rules* about the distance which we will ideally maintain between ourselves and other people. As part of growing up in a particular society, we develop clear ideas about what is an acceptable distance for different forms of interaction, and for different relationships. People in different relationships will signal their degree of closeness physically, by the distances they maintain between themselves and others. Lovers, for example, will sit very much closer together than will two friends, and they in turn will sit closer to one another than would two strangers sharing the same seat. The four main interpersonal distances which Hall identified are given in Table 2.

Intimate	Up to about eighteen inches
Personal	Up to about four feet
Social	Up to about twelve feet
Public	Up to about eighteen feet

Table 2 Interpersonal distances
(from Hall, 1968)

There are cultural rules about situations which require physical closeness, and those which don't. In Western society we would signal that we wanted to tell someone something secret or intimate, for example, by moving closer to them; but if we were consulting a stranger, for example asking them the time, we would maintain a considerable distance between us and them. The fact that these distances vary from culture to culture can produce some problems in personal interaction: Watson & Graves (1966) showed that what is considered to be a comfortable speaking distance in some Middle Eastern cultures, for example, is considered to be a very intimate distance in America. People from Middle Eastern cultures, like people from South American ones, also were more likely to stand face-to-face, and to touch the person that they were speaking to.

Touch is a powerful non-verbal signal, and one which is often perceived as being deeply meaningful. Jourard (1966) performed a study in which college students described which parts of the body could be touched by various groups of people. Opposite-sex friends were allowed the most body contact, but in general it was only considered acceptable for family members or same-sex friends to touch the hands or sometimes the shoulders of the other person. Henley (1977) showed how touch is often used as a signal of power and status: higher-status individuals, such as senior managers, would often place an arm across the shoulders of a lower-status employee, to signal approval or inclusiveness; but lower-status employees never initiated touch contacts.

Paralanguage

Paralanguage is all about the way that we say things. We don't just deliver words in a flat monotone – we bring in tones of voice, vocal 'fillers' like 'er' or 'um', and we vary the speed with which we speak. These are all non-verbal signals which accompany speech, and which help us to clarify what we mean, or to convey additional information to other people. Davitz & Davitz (1959) showed that we have eight clearly distinguishable patterns of voice, which indicate to people the different moods that we are in. The moods to which they correspond are: affection, anger, boredom, cheerfulness, impatience, joy, sadness and satisfaction.

The tone of voice that we use can also be a powerful non-verbal signal about how competent or authoritative we are. Apple *et al.* (1979) showed that speaking with a high-pitched voice is often seen as reducing the credibility of what we are saying. Media advisers to Margaret Thatcher put this finding to work when she gained power as Prime Minister of Britain in 1979. Studies of her interview style showed that she had consciously deepened her voice and slowed down her rate of speech, as a strategy for enhancing her media credibility.

The use of vocal 'fillers' in conversation, such as 'er' and 'um', also makes a difference to how what we are saying is perceived. Mahl (1963) showed that speech errors increase dramatically when we are nervous or uncertain of what we are saying, and they are often picked up by the other person as a non-verbal signal. Similarly, Erikson *et al.* (1978) set up a study of how people judged what was being said in a court setting, and showed that the use of phrases like 'you know', 'kind of' and 'I guess' seriously reduced the credibility of what the person had to say.

Dress

Dress has always been acknowledged as a powerful medium of communication. Much modern fashion in Western societies is concerned with projecting specific images, which make statements about what type of person the wearer is. Comprehension and interpretation of image in consumer societies is highly sophisticated – in a sense, people are trained in it from the moment they become aware of advertisements!

But dress is also used for other purposes. The uniform of a nurse or a security guard, for instance, makes clear statements about what that person does, and what social role they are playing. Religious figures often wear distinctive dress, and sometimes both religious and social beliefs are indicated by costume: for example, the wearing of the chador by women in some Muslim countries makes a statement about the role of women in those societies, as well as about religious belief.

Functions of non-verbal cues

Ekman & Friesen (1969) classified the functions of non-verbal signals into five categories: emblems, illustrators, affect displays, regulators and adaptors. Each of these categories reflects a differing function: we may at times use the same signals, but for quite a different purpose.

Emblems

Emblems are signals which have a distinct and well-defined meaning, and which stand for a specific idea or concept. A policeman's uniform or a technician's coat makes clear statements about social role and areas of responsibility. Specific gestures, like putting a finger to the lips to signal for quiet, also fall into this category. There are less obvious forms of emblems too: adopting a particular style of dress (for example dressing as a 'punk') may indicate a social role just as much as a uniform does. Since people respond to these cues unconsciously, they often exert a considerable influence on the nature of our social interactions with other people. Many people, for instance, like to adopt a fairly formal style of dress if they are in a position of responsibility, because they feel (consciously or unconsciously) that it helps to promote a professional, task-oriented approach to what is going on.

Illustrators

Illustrators are non-verbal actions which accompany speech, and which help to show the meaning or intention underlying what is being said. So a wry facial expression may serve as an illustrator to indicate a 'well, I don't necessarily agree with this but here it is anyway' attitude to what is being said; or a warm tone of voice may underline a statement of approval or an expression of sympathy. The amount that people use illustrators varies both from culture to culture, and from individual to individual; but Ekman & Friesen observed that, in everyday speech, illustrators seem to be used particularly often when the speaker is finding it hard to put their thoughts into words.

Affect displays

Affect displays reveal emotional states, although the term is used very loosely to include attitudes – 'states of mind' – as well. They can involve many different cues: body posture to signal depression, resignation or confidence; tone of voice to indicate irritation or friendliness; a new style of dress to indicate a fresh approach; agitating fingers or feet to indicate nervousness or impatience. Many affect displays are unconscious, particularly when they concern the less obvious parts of the body. Part of the training that the police receive in interviewing techniques, for example, includes becoming aware of the small movements of the feet and legs. Although people can control facial expressions or posture, they are often unaware of tapping a foot rapidly, or shifting the feet about.

Regulators

Regulators are non-verbal signals which are used to help social actions along. Eye-contact, as we have seen, is a powerful regulator of conversation: we use it to signal when we are listening, to check that a listener has understood or is still listening; and to 'hand over', the other person's turn to speak. This applies to the teaching situation, just as much as it does in other contexts: Beattie (1984) described a study of eye-contact in tutorials, showing in particular how skilled many students become at averting their gaze as the lecturer is coming to the end of an utterance, so that they can avoid catching the lecturer's eye and having to speak next!

Adaptors

Adaptors are non-verbal signals which are usually involuntary, personal behaviours, which we resort to at times of uncertainty. These might include biting your nails, fiddling with a ring or tapping your fingers. Essentially, adaptors are used to help someone to cope in a given situation. Many lecturers and teachers, for instance, develop ritualised adaptors, like clearing the throat in a certain way before speaking. This minor ritual helps them to cope with the teaching situation. Ekman suggested that many of these idiosyncratic behaviours are learned from childhood, and carry over into adult life without our really being aware of them.

As you will probably have noticed, any given type of non-verbal cue can serve several different functions. The most powerful ones, like tone of voice, eye-contact or facial expression, can serve as illustrators, affect displays or regulators, and we may use them interchangeably. Any social situation involves innumerable complex meanings, and non-verbal signals may be communicating messages on a number of different levels simultaneously.

The importance of non-verbal communication

Effective non-verbal communication is a skill, and like other skills, it becomes almost unconscious once we have mastered it. In fact, we tend to notice non-verbal communication only when it is wrong, or interrupted in some way. For example, people who are highly insecure or anxious sometimes develop a habit of avoiding eye-contact with other people – they find it threatening. Yet eye-contact forms a normal part of everyday interaction, and if you are talking with someone who avoids it, you may feel uneasy yourself.

Often, in such cases, other people are unaware of just what it is that is wrong: all they know is that the person is a bit 'strange', and that they don't feel comfortable talking with them. But that is usually enough to leave that person even more lonely and isolated than before. Argyle (1981) argued that such people are helped considerably by *social skills training*, which teaches them the basics of non-verbal communication in normal social interaction, so that their contact with other people is more positive.

We place a great reliance on non-verbal communication, and if the non-verbal content of a message isn't congruent with its verbal content, as a general rule we tend to ignore the verbal content and believe the non-verbal message. Argyle *et al.* (1971) asked actors to give a verbal message to research participants, while at the same time using a non-verbal style that contradicted it. For instance, if the words that the actor was saying were hostile or aggressive, the manner in which they said it might be friendly; or the other way round. They found that people were four times as likely to remember the non-verbal message than the words that were actually being said.

This is probably realistic. It's easy to tell lies using words, but it's much more difficult to lie non-verbally. Just think of how you feel when you have to talk to someone you don't like. Automatically your muscles will stiffen up – you won't be as relaxed as you are when you are with your friends. You will also find it harder to smile; and the smile that you do manage can be shown using micro-photography to involve different muscles from a genuine smile. It's our non-verbal communication which tends to give us away, not what we say.

Non-verbal episodes

As a general rule, the psychological study of non-verbal communication has been concerned with specific acts and actions, and the social functions which they might serve. But analysing social interaction in terms of small acts may not be all that helpful to understanding social interaction in the long run. Harré, in 1979, pointed out that in everyday life, social experience takes the form of whole, meaningful episodes, not isolated acts or actions.

We need to look at the whole context, including the people concerned, the ways in which they express themselves, the background to what is going on, the setting in which events are taking place, and so on. So, for instance, instead of just looking at individual utterances in conversations, Harré suggests that we should look at whole conversations in terms of their social meaning - for the participants and for other people too. Studying a single conversation out of context, Harré argued, isn't likely to tell us very much.

Ritual

One area of non-verbal communication which would require Harré's *ethogenic* approach of looking at episodes and accounts if we were to have any chance of making sense of what was going on, is the area of ritual. Ritual is a deeply meaningful form of communication in any human society; but it is about complete episodes, not individual acts or actions. And rituals can only really be understood when we look at the social meaning of what is going on.

So, for example, although the form of the ritual varies from one culture to another, every human society has rituals to deal with death and bereavement. These rituals play an important part in structuring the bereaved person's experience, and giving them a way of expressing their grief in a familiar, yet special, setting. By prescribing what should happen and when, a higher-order 'script' is imposed, which draws on any number of different verbal and non-verbal signals to make up a meaningful whole. A ritual forms a complete 'episode' of experience, and provides a framework within which that experience can be understood with the minimal amount of explanation.

Ritual serves an important function in social life, because it provides a clear structure within which interaction takes place. But ritual carries higher-order meanings too, and the nature of the ritual can tell us volumes about social organisation and power structures. The rituals associated with a formal examination, for instance, convey messages of distrust and suspicion. This distrust extends both to those conducting the examination (whose behaviour is rigidly prescribed by the regulations) and to the students taking the exams. For the most part, we perceive these messages unconsciously, but this doesn't mean that they are less powerful – in fact, unconscious messages of this kind can often be even more influential than messages of which we are consciously aware.

Everyday rituals

Berne (1973) identified a number of everyday rituals which people carry out. For example, a conversation involves verbal exchanges between two people. The formal rituals of religious ceremonies often also involve utterances and responses, although we wouldn't describe these as conversations in any ordinary sense. Yet many of our everyday conversations are almost as ritualised. Berne pointed out that many of the conversations which take place in everyday social life actually have a ritual function, rather than a straightforward communicative one: they serve to affirm participation in social life, rather than to communicate information.

For example, think of the 'How are you?' conversations which you have with acquaintances that you meet when you're out shopping, or at the bus stop. There is a definite pattern to the enquiries and replies, and there is also a prescribed context – you are supposed to respond in a particular way. Although these may seem to be simply examples of brief conversations, they really are not anything to do with exchanging information. Instead, they are all about reaffirming the social relationship.

Environmental messages

Take a fresh look at the layout of an average classroom or lecture theatre. In a typical classroom, the teacher – one person – has about one third of the space, while the students sit close together in the remaining two thirds. In a lecture theatre, the lecturer has a wide open area, while the students sit closely packed in tiers. In both locations the teacher is the one who has freedom to move about, whereas the students are expected to stay still, in one place. The room is arranged in a series of rows, such that the students sit side by side, and are more or less forced to face the teacher (a signal of attention). These are powerful non-verbal signals, which are saying things directly about relationships between teachers and the students.

One important message which they convey is that communication should be between teacher and student, and not between the students themselves. When we are talking to someone in everyday life – particularly if it is an intense or serious conversation – we tend to face the person that we're talking to, so that we can make eye-contact with them and signal that we are paying attention. In a typical classroom, eye-contact between students is made difficult by the physical layout, but eye-contact between teacher and student is made easy. Power and authority are also reflected in the relative amount of space which each person has. These environmental signals contribute directly to controlling the social interaction which goes on. That's why a teacher who is interested in group work will often rearrange the layout of the room: arranging chairs in small circles helps people to talk to one another more freely, and tends to lead to a better discussion.

Non-verbal messages, then, are not just transmitted by specific cues. There are non-verbal messages in the use of ritual or regularity, or the lack of it; in the proportion of positive to non-positive interactions within a group or pair of people; in the provision or lack of information in a working setting; in the physical layout of a room or building; and in many other aspects of experience. In fact, almost anything can, and does, serve as a non-verbal signal in social interaction! Symbolism is a crucially important part of everyday living. We can see from this that non-verbal communication operates on a number of levels, ranging from specific signals to more general messages about social assumptions. It is a major factor in how we perceive other people, and how we respond to them.

References

Apple W, Streeter LA & Krauss RM (1979) 'Effects of pitch and speech rate of personal attributions' *Journal of Personality and Social Psychology* 37: pp715–717

Argyle M (1975) *Bodily communication* Methuen

Argyle M (1981) 'The contribution of social interaction research to social skills training' in D Wine & MD Smye eds *Social competence* Guildford Press

Argyle M, Lalljee M & Cook M (1968) 'The effects on visibility on interactions in a dyad' *Human Relations* 21: pp3–17

Argyle M, Alkema F & Gilmour R (1971) 'The communication of friendly and hostile attitudes by verbal and non-verbal signals' *European Journal of Social Psychology* 1: pp385–402

Beattie G (1984) 'The threads of discourse and the web of interpersonal involvement' Spearman Medal Address, British Psychological Society

Berne E (1973) *Games people play* Penguin

Davitz JR & Davitz L (1959) 'Correlates of accuracy in the communication of feelings' *Journal of Communication* 9: pp110–117

Dovidio JF & Ellyson SL (1982) 'Decoding visual dominance: attributions of power based on relative percentages of looking while speaking and looking while listening' *Social Psychology Quarterly* 45: pp106–113

Eibl-Eiblesfeldt I (1972) 'Similarities and difference between cultures in expressive movements' in RA Hinde ed *Non-verbal communication* Cambridge University Press

Ekman P & Friesen WV (1969) 'The repertoire of non-verbal behaviour: categories, origins, usage and coding *Semiotica* 1: pp49–98

Ellsworth PC & Langer EJ (1976) 'Staring and approach: an interpretation of the stare as a non-specific activator' *Journal of Personality and Social Psychology* 33: pp117–122

Erikson BE, Lind A, Jonson BC & O'Barr WM (1978) 'Speech style and impression formation in a court setting: the effects of "powerful" and "powerless" speech' *Journal of Experimental Social Psychology* 14: pp266–279

Friedman HS, DiMatteo MR & Mertz TI (1980) 'Non-verbal communication on television news: the facial expression of broadcasters during coverage of a presidential election campaign' *Personality and Social Psychology Bulletin* 6: pp427–435

Hall ET (1968) 'Proxemics *Current Anthropology* 9: pp83–108

Harré R (1979) *Social Being* Basil Blackwell

Henley N (1977) *Body politics: power, sex and non-verbal communication* Prentice-Hall

Jourard SM (1966) 'An exploratory study of body accessibility' *British Journal of Social and Clinical Psychology* 5: pp221–231

Kendon A (1967) 'Some functions of gaze direction in social interaction' *Acta Psychologica* 26: pp22–63

Knapp ML, Hart RP & Dennis HS (1974) 'An exploration of deception as a communication construct' *Human Communication Research* 1: pp15–29

Lawick-Goodall JSVan (1974) *In the shadow of man* Collins

McGinley H, LeFevre R & McGinley P (1975) 'The influence of a communicator's body position on opinion change in others' *Journal of Personality and Social Psychology* 31: pp686–690

Mahl GF (1963) 'The lexical and linguistic levels in the expression of emotion' in PH Knapp ed *Expression of the emotions in man* International University Press

Osgood CE (1966) 'Dimensionality of the semantic space for communication via facial expression' *Scandinavian Journal of Psychology* 7: pp1–30

Watson ON & Graves TD (1966) 'Quantitative research in protemic behaviour' *American Anthropologist* 68: pp971–985